GREAT MOMENTS

in Baseball

GREAT MOMENTS
in Baseball

DAVID CRAFT

MetroBooks

MetroBooks

An Imprint of Friedman/Fairfax Publishers

Library of Congress Cataloging-in-Publication Data

Craft, David.
    Great moments in baseball / David Craft.
        p. cm.
    Includes bibliographical references (p.) and index.
    ISBN 1-56799-418-0
    1. Baseball—United States—History. 2.Baseball—United States—
    History—Pictorial works.   I. Title.
    GV863.AIC676   1997
    796.357 '64' 0973—dc21
                                            96-48672

Editor: Stephen Slaybaugh
Art Director: Kevin Ullrich
Designer: Galen Smith
Photography Editor: Wendy Missan

Color separations by HK Scanner Arts Int'l Ltd.
Printed in Singapore by KHL Printing Co Pte Ltd.

10 9 8 7 6 5 4 3 2 1

For bulk purchases and special sales, please contact:
Friedman/Fairfax Publishers
Attention: Sales Department
15 West 26th Street
New York, NY 10010
212/685-6610 FAX 212/685-1307

Visit our website:
http://www.metrobooks.com

Dedication

This book is dedicated to those who have had the greatest influence on my writing: my parents, Everett and Eunice Craft; my twelfth-grade composition-literature teacher, Jerry Wadden; and my first newspaper editor, Jim Potter.

CONTENTS

Shakespeare could well have been describing baseball players when he wrote that "some are born great, some achieve greatness, and some have greatness thrust upon them." Bill should know; he made some fine plays in his day—many of them dramatic—before enthusiastic crowds of all ages.

Of course, as he would quickly add, "great" does not always mean something that is good or grand. "Great" can describe something that is notable, remarkable, full of emotion—but not necessarily positive. That is why entries on the 1919 "Black Sox" scandal and Lou Gehrig's tearful farewell to baseball, as well as a short entry on the 1981 players' strike that ate up a third of the season, are included in this book. They don't elicit smiles from people, but they are major threads in baseball's rich fabric. And for fans of those teams on the short end of a game-winning hit or a game-saving catch, some of the great moments captured in this book may elicit sighs or winces.

But regardless of your team allegiance, this book will serve as a primer on many of big-league baseball's great moments in the twentieth century, particularly if your interest in baseball history is just now beginning.

This book gives you a flavor of the people—some famous, some infamous—who helped shape true events that have taken on folkloric proportions over the years. It's not surprising then that even someone as bright and talented as former Yankees slugger Don Mattingly once said of the legendary Sultan of Swat, "Honestly, at one time I thought Babe Ruth was a cartoon character. I really did. I mean, I wasn't born until 1961."

Indeed, the circumstances surrounding many of baseball's great moments seem so improbable to us today that our response is simply, "Wow!" or "I can't believe that really happened." So whether you're part of Don Mattingly's generation or part of another one, age doesn't matter. Baseball links the generations. This book is for you.

Kansas City Royals mainstay George Brett could do it all: hit for average, hit with power, run, field, and throw. The 1985 Gold Glove winner led the American League in hitting, slugging, triples, and total hits three times each, doubles twice, and on-base percentage once.

GM Branch Rickey's decision to integrate baseball with Jackie Robinson was both wise and fortunate. Robinson's character in the face of racial hatred justified Rickey's belief in his player as a man, and Robinson's athletic prowess spurred the signings of other African-American ballplayers who helped Rickey's Dodgers win pennants for many years afterward.

1901-1919: From an Uneasy Truce to a Postseason Debacle

Napoleon Lajoie had "bulked up" during the off-season. The pitching was generally poor. The ball was juiced. Napoleon's bat was corked. It was luck. It was magic.

It was 1901, and whatever the reason, Lajoie's home run total that year (14) was double that of his 1900 output. But the hitting sensation of the fledgling American League never again reached those lofty heights; he averaged about 3 homers a season for the next fifteen years.

In 1902, Pittsburgh Pirate Tommy Leach was tops in the National League with 6 home runs–and he had to scoot to get them, because every one was hit inside the park.

The 1906 Chicago White Sox hit only 6 home runs as a team. Two years later they hit only 3, and 1 was by 40-game-winning pitcher Ed Walsh. In fact, until 1919, the most homers hit by any player in either league in any season was 24.

Welcome to the deadball era.

Bats were generally much heavier than those in use today. To gain better control of the bat, a hitter would either grip the handle with his hands a few inches apart or choke up on the handle; some hitters did both. Generally taking a short stride, the hitter would go with the pitch and attempt to "push" or "punch" the ball rather than jack it over the fence. Materials used in the construction of the ball itself, combined with such remarkable pitchers as Cy Young, Walter Johnson,

Pitchers win the Cy Young Award based on what they accomplish over a single season. The irony is that Young himself was often overshadowed by his contemporaries in any given year. But from 1890 through 1911, he was the model of consistency and durability, pitching five 30-win seasons and fifteen 20-win seasons, and posting a 2.63 career ERA with 749 complete games.

Napoleon "Nap" Lajoie was an established star in the National League when he jumped to the fledgling American League for the 1901 season. He and fellow jumpers Cy Young, Jimmy Collins, John McGraw, and Joe McGinnity helped legitimize the new league. Lajoie was so popular with Cleveland fans that for several years the team was known as the Cleveland Naps.

Christy Mathewson, Mordecai Brown, Eddie Plank, Eddie Cicotte, Pete Alexander, Rube Waddell, Joe Wood, Jeff Pfeffer, Hippo Vaughn, Chief Bender, and Ed Reulbach, forced the team at bat to play what is called "inside baseball."

The sacrifice bunt, the hit-and-run or the run-and-hit, the stolen base, bunting for a hit, the squeeze play: a team's offense was based on these and other inside strategies.

But the deadball era was not deadly dull. It began with the bright promise of the American League's birth in 1901 and ended with the dark days of autumn 1919, when several players on the heavily favored White Sox tanked the World Series for a few thousand dollars from gamblers. In between those benchmarks were record-setting performances, thrilling pennant races, historic plays, and the larger-than-life exploits of many of the game's legends. In short, it was like any other time in baseball.

THE NATIONAL PASTIME MADE BETTER

With all of the highly publicized rancor over money between big-league owners and players in recent years, it seems inconceivable that at the start of this century there lived a baseball executive who circumvented the salary cap and paid top dollar to his players.

But throughout the 1890s Byron Bancroft Johnson, or "Ban" as he was known, had nurtured his dream of creating a second major league to rival the National League, which, since its formation in 1876, had been the principal element of professional baseball. The sportswriter-turned-businessman was president of the Western League, easily the strongest of the minor leagues at the turn of the century.

He focused on fixing the game's ills: drunkenness in the stands, rowdyism (among players as well as fans), loud profanity, and the disrespect players and managers openly showed for the

Fall Format Flip-Flop

....

The World Series began in 1903 with a best-of-nine-games format. When baseball's power brokers agreed to resume World Series play in 1905 after a one-year hiatus caused by the New York Giants' refusal to play the AL champions, the World Series was switched to a four-of-seven format. It stayed that way through 1918.

The best-of-nine format was reinstated for the 1919 season, and remained in place for the next two seasons as well. But it again gave way to the best-of-seven format that over the years had proved more popular with fans and players alike. That arrangement endures today.

New Yorkers who couldn't get tickets to the 1905 World Series games at the Polo Grounds could still see their beloved Giants take on the Philadelphia Athletics by standing atop Coogan's Bluff behind home plate. The Series lasted just five games. Each game was a shutout, and the Giants' Christy Mathewson hurled three of them, including the 2–0 clincher that took only ninety-five minutes to play.

umpires. He first brought about these changes in the Western League, which in 1900 he renamed the American League, and in 1901 took the liberty of bestowing major league status upon.

Sharing Johnson's vision was former player Charles Comiskey, who, by the late 1890s, was managing a franchise in the Western League. (He later owned the Chicago White Sox and became one of the game's more powerful and respected men.) The duo knew full well that the heads of the National League were going to take them to court in an effort to keep professional baseball the sole domain of the National League.

Johnson and Comiskey played hardball by ignoring the National Agreement, which governed all of organized baseball, and raided the National League of several top players, including Napoleon Lajoie and Cy Young. Over the next couple of years, Willie Keeler, Sam Crawford, and Jack Chesbro would jump to the American League. What's more, the upstart league placed three of its eight franchises in cities already occupied by NL teams: Boston, Chicago, and Philadelphia. (St. Louis was added in 1902, New York in 1903.) In those cities, the AL entries often outdrew their NL counterparts at the turnstiles. So, after a two-year

legal battle, the National League finally recognized Johnson's creation as a major league, and a new National Agreement was drawn up and ratified prior to the 1903 season.

The first White Sox manager was Clark Griffith. He later owned the Washington Senators, and was a major influence on the Roosevelt administration's decision to keep big-league baseball going in the 1940s despite blackout restrictions and America's commitment of manpower and materials to the war effort.

Over in Philadelphia, the Athletics were guided by owner-manager Cornelius McGillicuddy, better known as Connie Mack. In his fifty years at the helm, his teams won nine pennants and five World Series. His players included eventual Hall of Famers Home Run Baker, Chief Bender, Eddie Collins, Jimmie Foxx, Lefty Grove, Eddie Plank, Al Simmons, and Rube Waddell. Mack remains one of the game's more popular figures.

Mack, Clark Griffith, Charles Comiskey, and Ban Johnson, are enshrined in the Hall of Fame in Cooperstown as well. Their contributions to the game of baseball, spearheaded by the visionary Johnson, are still being felt as we head into the next millennium.

THE FIRST FALL CLASSIC—AND NEARLY THE LAST

The acrimonious dust had settled and an uneasy peace reigned between the two major leagues; the 1903 baseball season was underway, a season now remembered for one magical event: the first World Series.

Nearly a century later, this jewel still retains its luster.

Game One featured the first home run in World Series history. Pirates right fielder Jimmy Sebring, who had already singled twice and knocked in 3 runs, socked a homer well into the center field seats. Pittsburgh starter Deacon Phillippe struck out ten Boston Red Sox en route to a 7–3 victory. Cy Young took the loss. More than sixteen thousand mostly partisan fans witnessed the event at the Huntington Avenue Baseball Grounds.

Boston evened the series the next day when Patsy Dougherty smashed 2 homers and Bill Dinneen fired a 3-hitter to win 3-0.

Pirates manager Fred Clarke called on Phillippe to pitch Game Three, despite the pitcher

This is the scene prior to a 1903 World Series game at Boston's Huntington Avenue Baseball Grounds, home turf of the Red Sox; the franchise's name changed often and in other years they had been known as the Pilgrims, the Puritans, and the Somersets. It was common practice at the bandboxes of long ago for fans to line the outfield and perch atop the fence to see a game; this ballpark's seating capacity was only nine thousand.

Toast of the Town

· ·

The 1906 World Series pitted the Chicago Cubs, who won a record 116 games during the season, against the Chicago White Sox, whose team batting average of .230 testified to their nickname "the hitless wonders." But in true David-versus-Goliath fashion, the Sox toppled the heavily favored Cubs, 4 games to 2, despite batting only .198. On the other hand, Sox pitching limited the vaunted Cubs offense to a .196 batting average.

having had only one day of rest. Phillippe responded by allowing only 4 hits in a complete-game performance, and the Pirates won 4–2.

A travel day to Pittsburgh's Exposition Park was followed by a rainout, so Clarke again tabbed Phillippe as his starter. And again the righty came through with a complete game, winning 5–4 and shoving Boston into a 3-to-1 hole.

For Game Five, Boston went with its ace, Young, who answered the call with his bat as well as his arm: he drove in 3 runs (2 on a triple in Boston's 6-run uprising in the sixth inning) and gave up just 6 hits in an 11–2 Boston rout. The next day, Dinneen evened the series at 3 games apiece when he won, 6–3.

Pittsburgh's number three starter, Ed Doheny, was under a doctor's care for mental health problems and could not be called on by Pirates skipper Clarke. Sam Leever, the team's top pitcher during the regular season, and number four starter Brickyard Kennedy, had been shelled in their Series starts. Clarke was compelled to go with Phillippe for Game Seven. But "the Deacon" gave up 2 quick runs in the top of the first on a pair of Pirate triples and a dropped ball by his catcher, and Pittsburgh never recovered; the final was 7–3, and Boston moved ahead, 4 games to 3.

Game Eight was pushed back by rainy weather in Boston, giving Phillippe—this time working on two days' rest—another shot at victory. The game remained scoreless until the Boston fourth, when the home team scored 2 runs. Two innings later, Boston scored its third and final run of the game, and Dinneen cruised to a 4-hit shutout.

Boston, the best team in the upstart American League, had beaten the best the National League had to offer, 5 games to 3, in a championship series that featured a whopping 25 triples and a pair of 3-game winners: Dinneen and Phillippe. (Many of the triples resulted from a special ground rule that rated 3 bases for any ball going into the overflow crowd in the outfield.)

Casual observers may have thought the two rival leagues were headed toward a new era in organized baseball. After all, the 8-game postseason event was a great capper to a solid season. And as the 1904 season narrowed to a thrilling two-way race in the American League between the defending Boston Pilgrims and the pesky New York Highlanders, each club announced it would be willing to play the NL champion in a "world's championship" like the one staged the year before. There was a movement toward getting the National Commission, baseball's three-member governing board, to sanction the series and make it an annual ritual.

But John T. Brush and John J. McGraw, the owner and manager, respectively, of the NL champion New York Giants, snubbed the offer. There would be no world's championship in 1904. The official line from the Giants was that the American League was an inferior lot.

In reality, McGraw was fanning the fire that had grown between him and AL president Ban Johnson from several run-ins the two great egos (and former allies) had had when McGraw was player-manager of the AL Baltimore Orioles in 1901 and 1902. And Brush was still seething because there was now an AL club in New York City to compete with his Giants for the fans' hearts and wallets.

For their decision, the Giants got a noisy Bronx cheer not only from New Yorkers but the entire country as well. Stung by the criticism, Brush himself proposed a best-of-seven World

Yeah, but Could He Hit?

· ·

William Howard Taft became the President who set a precedent, when he threw out the first ball on Opening Day, April 14, 1910.

Series that would be held every year. Good timing on Brush's part. His Giants captured the 1905 NL pennant and beat the Philadelphia Athletics in the World Series, 4 games to 1. All 5 games were shutouts. Christy Mathewson won his 3 starts, and teammate Joe McGinnity notched the other Giants victory. A's ace Chief Bender got the lone opposition win.

The World Series was here to stay. Well, at least until 1994, when greed and egos once again got in the way.

DOWN TO THE WIRE IN BOTH LEAGUES

It is the mark of a great pennant race when the World Series is an anticlimax. Baseball fans in 1908 were treated to two great pennant races. The Detroit Tigers edged the Cleveland Indians by half a game and the Chicago White Sox by 1½ games to win their second consecutive AL crown, while the Chicago Cubs captured their third consecutive NL crown by outlasting the New York Giants and the Pittsburgh Pirates by a game each.

Rules in force at the time affected the outcomes of both races.

The Tigers lost their season opener to the White Sox, 15–5, despite Ty Cobb's 3-hit performance that included a home run into the right field bleachers at Chicago's South Side Park. The Tigers lost 9 of their first 12 games before righting themselves and winning 9 straight. As the season moved on, they found themselves in a four-way dogfight with those same White Sox, the Indians, and the surprising St. Louis Browns, whose pitching staff would compile the second best ERA in the league that year.

Despite the Giants fielding a team that included good-hitting outfielder Mike Donlin and pitching great Christy Mathewson, many observers had predicted the war for the NL flag would be waged by the Cubs and the Pirates. When the Giants played .500 ball for the first few

Opposite: In 1908, with a week to go in a red-hot AL pennant race, Cleveland's Addie Joss (right) pitched a 1–0 perfect game against Chicago's Ed Walsh (left), who gave up just 4 hits and struck out 15 batters. Joss' 1.16 ERA and Walsh's 40 wins were both tops in the majors that year, but neither man saw postseason action—the Detroit Tigers won the pennant by half a game over Cleveland and 1½ games over Chicago.

months of the season, it seemed those predictions would run true. But some of the other Giants, including thirty-seven-year-old Joe McGinnity, who chipped in with 11 wins, and outfielder Cy Seymour, who, despite hitting just .267, still knocked in 92 runs, helped New York stay in contention. By late September, the Giants were holding down first place.

The AL lead changed hands several times in the last two weeks of the season: Detroit was on top as of September 21; Cleveland, on September 22; then, a few days later, Detroit regained the top spot. In one game, Chicago ace Ed Walsh struck out fifteen Indians, but Cleveland won anyway because Walsh's mound opponent, Addie Joss, pitched a perfect game. But the very next day, Walsh came back with a win of his own, and a few days later won his fortieth game of the season by beating the Tigers while the Browns beat the Indians. With one game left to play, the Tigers led by half a game over Cleveland and Chicago.

Although Cleveland beat the Browns the next day, Detroit beat the Sox in Chicago. Under major league rules of that period, Detroit was not required to make up a game that had been rained out earlier in the season, so Cleveland, though they played all 154 of their games while Detroit only played 153, could draw no closer than half a game to Detroit, thereby losing the pennant by a margin of .004 percentage points.

The NL pennant race was just as wild. The morning papers of Wednesday, September 23, showed the Giants and Cubs in a virtual first-place tie in the standings, with the Pirates just 1½ games behind. The Cubs were in New York that day to play the Giants.

It was a pitchers' duel all the way, Mathewson going for the Giants and Jack Pfiester for the Cubs. With 2 out, 2 on, and the score tied at 1–1 in the bottom of the ninth, Giant Al Bridwell lined Pfiester's pitch to center and nearly decapitated umpire Bob Emslie, who was stationed near second base. The runner at first, rookie Fred Merkle, saw that teammate Harry McCormick had easily scored the winning run

from third. So, in the usual custom of the era, Merkle did not run all the way to second but instead trotted toward his team's clubhouse.

Cubs second baseman Johnny Evers yelled to his center fielder, Artie Hofman, to throw him the ball. With the ball in his possession, Evers could step on second base, forcing Merkle for the third out of the inning and nullifying McCormick's run. But when McCormick touched home plate, thousands of energetic Giants fans poured onto the field to celebrate their team's crucial victory over the hated Cubs. Hofman's relay to Evers was, depending on which version you accept, either intercepted by another Giant, who fired the ball into the stands, or simply lost in the mass of humanity now covering the infield. In any case, with players, fans, and police darting all over the place in wild confusion, Evers retrieved a ball and stepped on the bag at second. He ran to Emslie, who was heading off the field, but his appeal fell on deaf ears: the ump said he had been dodging Bridwell's liner, saw McCormick race home, and didn't see what Merkle did (or didn't do) after the ball was hit.

But later that evening, away from the playing field, home plate umpire Hank O'Day went by the rule book and declared Merkle out at second and the game a 1–1 tie, impossible to finish due to darkness and the swarms of people on the playing field. (Coincidentally, O'Day and Evers were both involved in a play three weeks earlier in a Cubs-Pirates game, but that time, O'Day, who was running off the field after he saw the base runner touch home plate, ruled against Evers and the Cubs.)

In the days that followed, the best protest the Giants could muster was a declaration by league officials that if the two teams ended the season in a dead heat, the tie game would be replayed.

At season's end on October 7, the Cubs and the Giants had identical records of 98–55. The next day the two rivals met in New York to decide the 1908 NL Championship. The Giants took an early lead, but the Cubs rallied for 4 runs in the third and held on to win the game and the pennant, 4–2.

All of baseball reflected on the tie game of September 23. Rules are rules, but Merkle ran the base paths as was customary for the day. Yet, fans and members of the press vilified him, calling the kid "Bonehead" and blaming him for New York's pennant debacle. It was a cold-blooded moniker that haunted him most of his life, despite several

In the old days, photographers could position themselves on the playing field, and in 1909, the legendary lensman Charles M. Conlon snapped his most famous action shot. Detroit's Ty Cobb steals third and upends New York Highlanders third baseman Jimmy Austin in the process.

Johnny Evers was considered one of the top-fielding second base-men in his day, but it was his baseball smarts as much as his glove work that propelled the Cubs past the Giants in the 1908 NL pennant race. Evers called for the ball and tagged second base for the third out in the legendary "Merkle play."

good years in the majors. Giants manager John McGraw, however, viewed Merkle as blameless, and even gave him a $500 raise for the following season.

That same season, NL president Harry Pulliam took his own life. He left no suicide note, but it was obvious to all who had contact with him that he had become increasingly despondent and withdrawn because of job stress in part related to severe criticism of his handling of the Merkle game.

TENTH-INNING TURNAROUND

Boston Red Sox hurler Smokey Joe Wood clearly enjoyed a career year in 1912. He went 34–5 with a 1.91 ERA and a league-leading 10 shutouts, and he hit .290 with 15 extra-base hits and 13 runs batted in. The Sox outdistanced their nearest challenger, the Washington Senators, by 14 games to win the AL pennant.

Their opponents in the World Series were the New York Giants, whose pitching staff led the majors in ERA and whose lineup led the majors in batting average and home runs.

The Series was a dandy. With the exception of Game Two—a 6–6 tie that was called after 11 innings because of darkness—and Game Seven—an 11–4 New York win (and Wood's only loss)—every game was decided by 1, 2, or 3 runs.

Knotted at 3 games apiece, the Red Sox and Giants battled for baseball's crown on Wednesday, October 16, at Boston's Fenway Park, which was in its first year of operation. Boston's Hugh Bedient and New York's Christy Mathewson, the winner and loser, respectively, of Game Five, were the starting pitchers.

The Giants drew first blood when Red Murray doubled home Josh Devore in the third. Two innings later, the Giants were robbed of a home run when Red Sox right fielder Harry Hooper lit out for right-center field, leaped, and snared Larry Doyle's booming liner just as the ball

The Double No-Hitter

· ·

The date was May 2, 1917, and through 9 innings, neither Cincinnati Red Fred Toney nor Chicago Cub Jim Vaughn had given up a hit. But the Reds tallied an unearned run off Vaughn in the top of the tenth and Toney mowed the Cubs down in the bottom of the tenth to preserve his 1–0 no-hit victory.

was sailing into the temporary bleachers. Boston tied the score in its half of the seventh on a run-scoring double by pinch hitter Olaf Henriksen.

The score was frozen at 1–1 going into the top of the tenth. But a double by Murray and a single by Fred Merkle put the Giants ahead by a run. In the bottom of the frame, light-hitting utility man Clyde Engle pinch-hit for Wood, who had relieved Bedient in the eighth. (Wood was unable to bat for himself because he injured his right hand when he fielded a smash off the bat of Chief Meyers and threw him out at first base to end the Giants rally.) Engle skied a Mathewson pitch into center field, where Fred Snodgrass camped under the ball—and dropped it. Engle, hustling all the way, took second on the 2-base error. Snodgrass then made a superb running catch of Hooper's shot to deep center.

After Mathewson walked Steve Yerkes, Tris Speaker stepped up to the plate. He hit a pop foul near first base that was Merkle's play to make. When Merkle didn't break for the ball, catcher Meyers vainly ran up the line to pull it in. But the ball fell in no-man's-land near the first-base coach's box. Given new life, Speaker then lined a single to right that scored Engle with the tying run and sent Yerkes to third with the potential winning run. Speaker took second on the throw to the cut-off man. Duffy Lewis was intentionally walked to set up a force at any base. But Larry Gardner

No telling what "Smokey" Joe Wood might have accomplished on the mound if he hadn't hurt his pitching arm at the age of twenty-three. In the five seasons before his injury, he racked up an 81–43 record with an ERA around 2. His 1912 campaign was capped by 3 victories in the World Series against the New York Giants. Wood's hitting prowess kept him in the big leagues after his pitching days were over, and he forged seasons of .296, .297, and .366 at the plate.

foiled the Giants' strategy by smacking a long sacrifice fly to right that easily scored Yerkes from third with the winning run.

It was a heartbreaking loss for the Giants, who had been up a run, while the Red Sox enjoyed the excitement of coming back from being down by 1 run to win. What a game! And for Smokey Joe Wood, the 3–2 final gave him his third victory of the Series.

FADE TO BLACK

Most of the thirty thousand fans packed into Cincinnati's Redland Field on that Wednesday afternoon in autumn 1919 thought the game began when Chicago's Shano Collins led off the top of the first by stroking a single to center.

But to other observers—including eight of Collins' teammates—the game *really* began when Chicago starter Eddie Cicotte plugged Cincy's Morrie Rath in the back to lead off the bottom of the first.

That was the signal to the gamblers and the eight players involved that their fix of the 1919 World Series was on. Rath eventually scored, and the Reds went on to rout the heavily favored White Sox 9–1 in Game One. The Reds also won Games Two, Four, Five, and Eight to capture the best-of-nine Series, while the White Sox—largely on the heart and the pitching arm of little Dickie Kerr, who was not in on the fix—won Games Three, Six, and Seven.

Cicotte's coconspirators were fellow hurler Lefty Williams, left fielder and cleanup hitter Joe Jackson, first baseman (and ringleader) Chick Gandil, shortstop Swede Risberg, center fielder Happy Felsch, and utility infielder Fred McMullin. The eighth man, third baseman Buck Weaver, knew of the fix but refused to play along;

Opposite: New York Giants rookie Fred Merkle ran the bases like many players did back in 1908, but it cost him and his team dearly when sharp-eyed Johnny Evers of the Chicago Cubs appealed to the umpiring crew in a game whose outcome affected the NL pennant race that year. Right: His most famous pitch was a screwball, but Christy Mathewson himself always had a clear head. A dominating pitcher in an era when pitching was king, "Matty" won 94 games over a three-year span (1903–1905) and 373 games lifetime. He joined the army after his career was over, and though he was sent to France after World War I ended, Matty was somehow exposed to poison gas that weakened his lungs. He later contracted tuberculosis, from which he died in 1925 at the age of forty-five.

through a misguided sense of loyalty to his team-mates, he remained silent until September 1920, when one of the gamblers broke open the scandal by giving his account of the whole sorry mess to a Philadelphia newspaper. After that, Weaver and the others had to give testimony to a Cook County, Illinois, grand jury.

The eight were suspended by White Sox owner Charles Comiskey. Then they were brought to trial on conspiracy charges. The case ended in a mistrial when some crucial evidence mysteriously disappeared. Although the eight were acquitted in their second trial in 1921, newly elected Baseball Commissioner Judge Kenesaw Mountain Landis, in a sweeping move to clean up the game and restore people's faith in it, permanently banned the eight from baseball. They have been forever labeled as the Black Sox, and the episode itself is called the Black Sox scandal.

Ironically, the eight received little more than half of the $100 thousand the gamblers had promised them. And strange as it may seem, "Shoeless" Joe Jackson led all hitters in the Series with a .375 batting average and also hit the Series' only home run—odd for a man who had accepted a $5,000 bribe.

People often use the word "great" to describe something noble in character, something grand or distinguished. But great can also mean remarkable in magnitude. Certainly it is the latter meaning that applies to the tainted 1919 World Series, because nobility of character is precisely what these eight big-league ballplayers lacked.

The strikes of 1981 and 1994 were painful and maddening, and the on-field death of Ray Chapman in 1920 was tragic, but by far the ugliest chapter in baseball history was the throwing of the 1919 World Series by a handful of Chicago White Sox players. When the scandal was brought to light in 1920, it further underscored the need for a strong, impartial executive to oversee the national pastime. In January 1921, Judge Kenesaw Mountain Landis took office as baseball's first commissioner, a post he kept until his death in 1944. The eight players Landis banned from baseball are pictured as follows: Eddie Cicotte (front row, third from left), Lefty Williams (front row, second from right), Happy Felsch (middle row, third from right), Chick Gandil (middle row, second from right), Buck Weaver (middle row, right), Swede Risberg (back row, fifth from left), Fred McMullin (back row, fifth from right), and Joe Jackson (back row, second from right).

1920-1941: From the Bronx Bombers to Wartime Bombers

Babes on Broadway or the Babe in the Bronx? Harry Frazee had to choose.

Frazee, a New York–based theatrical producer who also owned the Boston Red Sox, was in a financial bind. He owed money, he needed fresh capital to pursue new possibilities in the entertainment industry, and his star player on the Red Sox, George Herman "Babe" Ruth, was demanding his salary be doubled in 1920 to $20,000 a year.

Enter the New York Yankees, who had their corporate headquarters just a few doors down from Frazee's theatrical office. During the 1919 season, Frazee and the Yankees ownership struck a deal that sent Red Sox pitcher Carl Mays to the Yankees for two players and $40,000. In early January of 1920, another deal between the two teams sent Ruth to the Yankees for the then whopping sum of $125,000. Frazee had his capital, and the Yankees had a legend in the making.

Ruth was a twenty-five-year-old slugger disguised as a pitcher when he suited up in Yankee pinstripes for the 1920 campaign. In his six-year stint with the Red Sox he had gone 89–46 with an earned run average around 2, but he was a master batsman as well. In 1919, his last year in Boston, he pounded out 29 homers, 12 triples, and 34 doubles; knocked in 114 runs; and hit .322.

For the Yankees he slugged 54 home runs in 1920, 59 in 1921, and 60 in 1927, the year of Lou Gehrig, Bob Meusel, Earle Combs, and the rest of "Murderers' Row." Ruth went on to set single-season and career home run and slugging records before hanging up his spikes in 1935.

The deadball era was dead. Long live the age of the long ball.

But the Roaring Twenties and the Depression thirties, while best remembered for gaudy batting

It's the bottom of the first in Game Four of the 1920 World Series, and Bill Wambsganss scores the first run in what would be Cleveland's 5–1 win over Brooklyn. The Brooklyn catcher is Otto Miller, who, thanks to Wambsganss, would be even more nonplused the next day. The home plate umpire is Bill Dinneen.

averages and home run totals reaching the stratosphere, produced some stellar pitching as well. Waite Hoyt, Dazzy Vance, Stan Coveleski, Lefty Grove, Dizzy Dean, Carl Hubbell, Lon Warneke, Bob Feller, Schoolboy Rowe, Red Ruffing, and Paul Derringer were just a few of the top guns on the mound during this period.

And, as the 1930s droned on, great hitters such as Johnny Mize, Joe DiMaggio, Ted Williams, Hank Greenberg, and Jimmie Foxx electrified a baseball-loving nation.

But by the mid-1940s, hundreds of big-league ballplayers, including several of the pitchers and hitters mentioned here, were wearing uniforms issued by Uncle Sam. World War II was raging on many fronts, and military service, not baseball, was uppermost in the players' minds. Some players took stateside duty; others went overseas. At least two big-league ballplayers from this era, Elmer J. Gedeon and Harry O'Neill, died in combat during World War II. Another, Bob Neighbors, died in North Korea in 1952.

The two decades preceding World War II produced many of the game's biggest names. There was also a one-of-a-kind fielding play in the postseason, consecutive no-hitters thrown by the same pitcher, and a tearful farewell to the iron man of baseball.

"Wamby" Wows 'Em

The stench from the 1919 World Series wafted through the air when the Cleveland Indians and Brooklyn Robins took the field on October 5, 1920.

It was Game One of the 1920 World Series, but in the weeks leading up to the Fall Classic, newspapers around the country broke the sordid story of how several unnamed Chicago White Sox players—promised big money by powerful gamblers—threw the 1919 World Series. The heavily favored White Sox lost that best-of-nine series to the Cincinnati Reds, 5 games to 3.

In Illinois, a Cook County grand jury convened on September 21 to hear testimony about the allegations and rumors that baseball was rife with gambling and crookedness, and the investigation quickly focused on the 1919 World Series.

This off-field discord was in sharp contrast to the breathtaking AL pennant race between the

Three's a Crowd-pleaser

....

Through the 1995 season there have been nine unassisted triple plays in addition to the one that Bill Wambsganss turned in the 1920 World Series. Wambsganss is one of two second basemen to perform this rare defensive gem; first basemen have done it twice, shortstops have done it six times, and no third basemen have done it. Wambsganss is the only player to ever do it in the Fall Classic.

Bill Wambsganss remains the only big-leaguer in history who could tell family and friends about making an unassisted triple play in the World Series. Perhaps the real oddity of the second baseman's feat is that with two men on base and his team ahead 7–0, he was playing deep for the relief pitcher, who was allowed to bat for himself.

The finale to one of baseball's legendary fielding gems is forever captured in this photo: Indians second baseman Bill Wambsganss tags Brooklyn runner Otto Miller for the third out of Wambsganss' unassisted triple play in the fifth inning of Game Five of the 1920 World Series. Making the call at second is umpire Hank O'Day. Looking on are (left to right) third base umpire Bill Dinneen, Brooklyn runner Pete Kilduff (whom Wambsganss had doubled off second), and Indians third baseman Larry Gardner. The first out came when Wambsganss snagged a liner off the bat of relief pitcher Clarence Mitchell.

White Sox and the Cleveland Indians. The Sox trailed the Indians by 1½ games when they opened a 3-game series at Cleveland on September 23. Cleveland's lone victory was sandwiched between 2 Sox wins.

Now just a half game out of first place, the Sox rode the train back to Chicago to play the Detroit Tigers in a Sunday afternoon game. It mattered little that the Sox won that game, because winning pitcher Eddie Cicotte and seven of his teammates were soon suspended by White Sox owner Charles Comiskey after they'd been publicly implicated in the 1919 World Series scandal. Without 20-game winners Cicotte and Lefty Williams, and the torrid hitting of outfielder Joe Jackson (a .382 average, 121 RBI, 42 doubles, and a league-leading 20 triples), the Sox sputtered in the final week and the Indians clinched the pennant by 2 games.

The 1920 Indians themselves were not without tragedy. On August 16 at the Polo Grounds in New York, the skull of Indians shortstop Ray Chapman was crushed by a high hard one that got away from Yankees submarine pitcher Carl Mays. The popular Chapman, hitting .303 at the time, never regained consciousness, and died the next day—the only on-field fatality in major league baseball history.

Cleveland player-manager Tris Speaker encouraged his players to put their hearts into the pennant race. Still dealing with their sorrow, they somehow regrouped for a final run at the AL title. The addition of two kids, Joe Sewell—Chapman's replacement at shortstop—and pitcher Walter "Duster" Mails, was key in bringing the pennant to Cleveland. In the final three weeks of the season, Sewell hit .329 with 12 runs batted in, and Mails was a perfect 7–0 with a 1.85 earned run

average in September. Speaker himself had a superb year, hitting .388 with 107 RBI and a league-leading 50 doubles. And then there was spitballer Stan Coveleski, who won 24 games and led the league in strikeouts.

But it was light-hitting second baseman Bill Wambsganss, a former seminarian, who stole the headlines during the Cleveland-Brooklyn World Series. The teams were tied at 2 games apiece in the best-of-nine event when they met for Game Five at Cleveland's League Park on October 10. The nearly twenty-seven thousand fans on hand for that Sunday afternoon contest saw a first in the first inning. In the bottom half of the inning, Cleveland's Charlie Jamieson singled to right. Then Wambsganss singled to center. Speaker reached first after putting down a dandy bunt that Brooklyn starter Burleigh Grimes couldn't field cleanly. With the bases loaded and no one out, cleanup hitter Elmer Smith pasted a 2-strike spitball over the right field fence for a grand slam— the first in World Series history.

Another World Series first exploded in the bottom of the fourth. Cleveland starter Jim Bagby, who won 31 games during the regular season, socked a 3-run homer that landed in the temporary seating in center field—the first home run by a pitcher in World Series play. That put the Indians ahead, 7–0.

For most performers, those heroics would be tough acts to follow. But Cleveland's Bill Wambsganss, whose name had to be shortened to "Wamby" to fit into newspaper box scores, was about to outshine them all.

Second baseman Pete Kilduff led off the Brooklyn fifth with a single to left-center field. Catcher Otto Miller followed with a single to center, Kilduff stopping at second. Clarence Mitchell, who had relieved Grimes after Bagby socked his homer, was allowed to hit for himself. Mitchell wasn't a slugger, but he was no slouch at the plate, either. With a 7-run lead, the Cleveland infielders played back for the double play. What they got was something more.

Mitchell smashed a line drive that was rising when Wambsganss took a step to his right and leaped into the air. He snared the ball in his gloved left hand while his momentum carried him toward second base. Wambsganss stepped on the bag to double up Kilduff, who had darted for third at the crack of the bat. Gripping the ball in his right hand

"Murderers' Row" was the catchy phrase newspaper reporters originally used to describe the heart of the 1927 New York Yankees' lineup—Babe Ruth, Lou Gehrig, Tony Lazzeri, Bob Meusel, and Earle Combs—that terrorized opposing pitchers. Over the years the phrase has come to emcompass the entire team, and for good reason. The '27 Yanks led the American Legue in nearly all major ofensive categories and the pitching staff boasted the lowest ERA total in the majors.

Four innings later, it was over. In their 8–1 win, the Indians also turned three double plays. Mitchell hit into one of them, which meant that two swings of his bat accounted for 5 outs that day.

The Indians also won the next 2 games at home—on shutouts by Mails and Coveleski—to clinch the Series, 5 games to 2. Coveleski's win was his third of the Series.

Perhaps, from a psychological standpoint, it was that fifth-inning fielding gem in Game Five that kept the Brooklyn club from bouncing back. Bill "Wamby" Wambsganss remains the only player to have made an unassisted triple play in the World Series.

No Contest

Preseason predictions for the 1927 baseball campaign generally trumpeted an exciting AL pennant race among as many as five of the eight teams in the junior circuit.

But when the dust had settled 154 games later, the New York Yankees had outdistanced their nearest challenger, the Philadelphia Athletics, by 19 games, and in the process set the single-season record for winning percentage: .714. The Yankees then swept the Pittsburgh Pirates in the World Series.

So much for preseason predictions.

Why were the '27 Yanks so good? What transformed them from the defending AL champions and a threat to repeat in 1927 into the legendary Murderers' Row?

Babe Ruth's 60 homers didn't hurt. Nor did Lou Gehrig's 175 runs batted in. And then there was the pitching staff led by 22-game winner Waite Hoyt. But many teams over the years have boasted a couple of big guns in the middle of the lineup and a mound ace or two but failed to win a pennant. No, the reason the 1927 Yanks murdered their rivals was that many of the players had career years.

Take, for example, the pitching staff. In Hoyt (22–7; .759), Urban Shocker (18–6; .750), Wilcy Moore (19–7; .731), and Herb Pennock (19–8; .704), the Yanks had the league's four best won–lost percentages. Rookie George Pipgras also had a winning percentage above .700 with his 10–3 record. And veteran Dutch Ruether, in his last big-league season, chipped in with 13 wins (against only 6 losses) and a 3.38 ERA. Yankee hurlers held

for a possible throw to first base to catch the other runner, Wambsganss quickly turned to see where Miller was. As it turned out, the stunned catcher was paralyzed a few feet from second base. Wambsganss tagged the dumbfounded runner for the third out.

The play took seconds to unfold. But once the fans realized that they'd just witnessed an unassisted triple play, they erupted into cheers for the steady but unheralded Wambsganss. The Cleveland dugout was full of whooping and hollering well-wishers, too.

Station to Station

·····························

Harold Arlin was at the mike when Pittsburgh radio station KDKA did the first broadcast of a baseball game, a Pirates win over the Philadelphia Phillies on August 5, 1921. On August 26, 1939, station W2XBS in New York was the first to televise a big-league game. However, few home viewers saw the Cincinnati Reds–Brooklyn Dodgers contest at Ebbets Field due to the lack of proliferation of televisions at this time.

the three top spots in the league's ERA standings. The staff gave up the fewest number of hits and the fewest number of walks in posting a league-low ERA of 3.20. And Moore, in addition to his 19 wins, tied for the league lead in saves with 13.

The '27 Yanks were outstanding glove men as well. Their .969 fielding percentage wasn't far behind Chicago's .971 clip, and only Chicago and Philadelphia committed fewer errors.

But it was with their bats that Murderers' Row forged a baseball legend. In addition to Ruth's 60 homers, Gehrig contributed 47 and Tony Lazzeri, 18. In addition to Gehrig's 175 runs batted in, Ruth contributed 164; Bob Meusel, 103; and Lazzeri, 102. Earle Combs led the league in hits with 231 and triples with 23. Gehrig was second in the league in hits with 218, second in batting average at .373, and first in doubles with 52.

As a team, the Yankees led the American League in nearly every major offensive category except for doubles and stolen bases. The team batting average was .307; the team slugging average, .489.

For the regular season the Pirates boasted six .300 hitters in their everyday lineup, a 22-game winner and a pair of 19-game winners on their pitching staff, and a solid bench that included Kiki Cuyler's .309 batting average, 20 stolen bases, and nearly two dozen extra-base hits.

In his twelve years with the New York Yankees, he often performed in the shadows of such titans as Babe Ruth, Lou Gehrig, and Joe DiMaggio, but second baseman Tony Lazzeri put together a solid big-league career that included a .292 lifetime average and nearly 1,200 runs batted in. This photo was taken in 1928, a season in which Lazzeri hit .332 with 82 RBI in 116 games despite suffering a shoulder separation.

But the triple-threat Yanks lived up to their reputation by outhitting (.279 to .223), outpitching (2.00 to 5.19), and outfielding (3 errors to 6) the scrappy Pirates to sweep the four-game Series.

The 1927 season was no contest.

THE BABE MAKES A POINT

To say there was bad blood between the 1932 Chicago Cubs and New York Yankees at World Series time is putting it mildly; bile and venom say it better.

The hostilities were twofold. First, there was the revenge factor: Yankees manager Joe McCarthy had piloted the Cubs to a NL pennant in 1929, only to be fired with about a week left in the 1930 season, when it was obvious the Cubs would not repeat as champs. Beating his former team would be sweet indeed.

Second, the late-season acquisition of former Yankees shortstop Mark Koenig had been pivotal in the Cubs' stretch drive. Koenig batted .353 in the last 30 games of the season. Yet the Cubs elected to give Koenig only a half share of the pennant money, and announced he would get the same for the Cubs' World Series take. Babe Ruth openly called the Cubs cheapskates, and other Yankees chimed in with their own epithets. The Cubs countered with a barrage of put-downs, most of them directed at Ruth, throughout the Series. Even the fans in the host cities joined in the vicious verbal fray.

The Yankees won the first 2 games at home by the scores of 12–6 and 5–2. Game Three in Chicago is remembered less for New York's 7–5 win than for what Ruth did—or didn't do—in the fifth inning. The slugger had already clubbed a 3-

Left: He was surly and quarrelsome, but Lefty Grove "could throw a lamb chop past a wolf," as prize-winning journalist Westbrook Pegler said. In 1928, the hard-throwing Grove twice struck out a side with nine pitches—one of these sides being the defending world champion "Murderers' Row" Yankees. Grove's fastball had no hop or sail to it; he simply fired it past most hitters. His best season was 1931, when he went 31–4 with a 2.06 ERA and 175 strikeouts—all tops in the majors that year. Lifetime he notched 300 wins. Opposite: Home runs, like laughter, can be infectious. Here, Lou Gehrig (4) congratulates teamate Babe Ruth after "The Bambino" crushed his second home run of Game Three. Seconds later Gehrig hit *his* second home run of the game. Ruth's homer was particularly satisfying as it silenced the Cubs bench jockeys. Pointing towards them, Ruth is believed to have called the shot.

run homer in the first inning (and Lou Gehrig had followed with a solo shot in the third). But the Cubs battled back to knot the score at 4–4. With 1 out in the top of the fifth, Ruth faced Cubs starter Charlie Root with the bases empty.

Root's first pitch was a called strike. The crowd roared and the Cubs' bench jockeys really laid into Ruth, who stared at the Cubs bench while he raised the index finger of his right hand as if to say, "That's only strike one." Root's next two pitches missed the mark, but the fourth pitch was another called strike to even the count. Again the Cubs players yelled at Ruth, and once again he gestured toward them—this time by holding up two fingers and pointing. Some accounts also say that he made a sweeping motion with his arm. Cubs fans were in a frenzy; Ruth and Root were jawing at each other.

Root's next pitch was a change-up curve, and Ruth walloped it. The ball landed well back in the center field bleachers. The Babe was ecstatic as he rounded the bases, and if his go-ahead clout didn't suck the wind out of Wrigley Field, then what happened to Root's very next pitch certainly did: Gehrig belted his second solo homer of the game, the ball landing in the temporary bleachers in right field. The Yanks held on to win, 7–5.

Did Ruth call his shot? Did he point to the bleachers and then park Root's curveball right

where he had pointed? Fans, the press, historians, the ballplayers—even the Yankees—could never agree on what happened that day. Ruth himself was tickled by the legend that formed around that homer, but he changed his story several times over the years.

Perhaps the victim should get the last word. Had Ruth gestured that he would hit the next pitch into the stands for a home run, Root said that Ruth "would have ended up on his ass" from a knockdown pitch.

Either way, the Babe made a point and New York swept the Series the next day.

THE IRON HORSE CALLS IT A CAREER

"Biscuit Pants" was an early nickname for the man who, years later, stood bowed at the microphone and with a heavy heart spoke the immortal words, "Today I consider myself the luckiest man on the face of the earth."

Lou Gehrig likely earned the moniker from bench jockeys who observed the six-foot (1.8m), two-hundred-pound (90.8kg) first baseman in his bulky, hot wool uniform, and decided the comparison was apt. But he was simply Lou to most of his teammates and, because he racked up Hall of Fame numbers while establishing a consecutive games played record that remained unbroken for fifty-six years, "the Iron Horse" to the world at large.

Gehrig was dying when he spoke those words, which have since become baseball's best remembered, reading from a self-penned speech that he delivered at Yankee Stadium during Lou Gehrig Appreciation Day on July 4, 1939.

In mid-June of that year, Gehrig had entered the Mayo Clinic in Rochester, Minnesota, to learn why his health had been deteriorating for many months. Gehrig voluntarily took himself out of the lineup on May 2. He had played in 2,130 consecutive big-league games. After performing a week-long series of tests and examinations on the slugger, clinic doctors announced their diagnosis: amyotrophic lateral sclerosis.

ALS is a rare, progressive, degenerative disease that attacks the body's central nervous system. Even for a strong, healthy athlete such as Lou Gehrig, the muscles atrophy over time, and paral-

ysis sets in. ALS itself is painless. It is also fatal. The doctors told Lou's wife, Eleanor, that her husband had, at best, about two years to live, news which she ultimately chose not to share with the Yankee great. Still, Gehrig knew he was meeting the toughest challenge of his life.

He remained with the Yankees throughout the 1939 season, sort of an unofficial "bench coach" for a team that, even without its all-star first baseman and team captain, was still very much a pennant contender. (In fact, the Yankees not only won the AL crown by a whopping 17-game margin over the Boston Red Sox, they blanked the Cincinnati Reds in 4 games to claim their fourth straight World Series.)

Acknowledging the outpouring of public sympathy for Gehrig, Eleanor, Lou's parents, and the Yankees' front office made preparations for Lou Gehrig Appreciation Day ceremonies to be held between games of a doubleheader against the Washington Senators on Independence Day at Yankee Stadium.

In addition to the current band of Bronx Bombers, many of Lou's former mates were on hand for the Tuesday afternoon tribute. Of the latter group, the presence of the now retired Babe Ruth, with whom Lou had endured an up-and-down relationship over the years, underscored the significance of the day. Remarks, often emotionally tinged, from several men, including Yankees manager Joe McCarthy, eventually gave way to the man of the hour.

Lou was at first too choked up to speak over the PA system. But when he heard a chorus of "We want Gehrig! We want Gehrig!" from most of the sixty-two thousand people in the stands, Lou composed himself and cautiously walked up to the microphone.

Cap in hand, he waited briefly for the stands to quiet down. Without slurring his words or becoming unsteady on his feet, the Iron Horse delivered a heartfelt address that he had written down but which he gave from memory.

In his address, Gehrig cited McCarthy's managerial wisdom, the honor of playing for Yankees owners Jacob Ruppert and Ed Barrow, his parents' work ethic, and his wife's strength. He talked about the kindnesses that people had shown him throughout his career, and his good fortune in having played major league baseball with many of the men present that day. Gehrig ended with, "So I close in saying that I might have had a bad break, but I have an awful lot to live for. Thank you."

A rolling thunder of approval swelled from the stands, and Ruth stepped forward and embraced his former teammate. It was a moment of healing for both men.

In the time he had remaining, Lou Gehrig served on the New York Parole Commission, was inducted into the National Baseball Hall of Fame, saw the Yankees retire his uniform number, caught a few games during the team's home stands, visited with friends and family, and generally tried to live as normal and fulfilling a life as his rapidly deteriorating body would allow. Throughout his ordeal, Lou remained mentally sharp and usually succeeded in putting up a brave front around well-wishers.

The Iron Horse died in his sleep on June 2, 1941. Two years and a month earlier, on the emotionally charged day that Gehrig took himself out of the lineup because he thought he was "hurting the club," pitcher Lefty Gomez quipped to his teammate, "Hell, Lou, it took them fifteen years to get you out of the ball game. Sometimes they get *me* out of there in fifteen minutes."

What a Year: Joe's 56, Ted's .406, and a Dropped Third Strike

On Thursday, May 15, 1941, Yankees outfielder Joe DiMaggio cracked a run-scoring single off Chicago White Sox left-hander Edgar Smith at Yankee Stadium. That productive but modest hit off the bat of "the Yankee Clipper" turned out to be the start of what many historians and fans still agree will be a tough record to break: hitting in 56 consecutive big-league games.

In today's vernacular, the twenty-six-year-old DiMaggio was "in a groove" for much of the 1941 season. But no one—not the press, not the fans, certainly not DiMaggio himself—talked much about his hitting streak in the early going. DiMaggio hit in his nineteenth straight game on June 2, the day his former teammate Lou Gehrig died of ALS.

By mid-June, DiMaggio closed in on Rogers Hornsby's NL record of hitting in 33 consecutive games; when he moved past Hornsby on June 21,

Down on the field, Lou Gehrig, Yankees manager Joe McCarthy, and members of the 1939 Senators are among those listening to one of the speakers during Lou Gehrig Appreciation Day at Yankee Stadium on July 4, 1939.

DiMaggio set his sights on the modern major league record of 41, held by St. Louis Brown George Sisler. DiMaggio doubled in the first game of a June 29 doubleheader at Washington against the Senators to tie Sisler's record. But before the start of the second game, someone sneaked into the Yankees dugout and took DiMaggio's favorite bat. By the seventh inning, DiMaggio was hitless. But he borrowed right fielder Tommy "Old Reliable" Henrich's bat and with it smacked a single to left to overtake Sisler in the record books.

DiMaggio then went after the big one: the 44-game streak set in 1897 by Willie Keeler, the man whose credo was "Hit 'em where they ain't." Joe hit one "where they can't go"—a home run into the left field bleachers at Yankee Stadium on July 2 to set a new all-time record.

Yet DiMaggio never let up. He continued his torrid hitting through July 16, when he lined a double and 2 singles to help the Yanks beat the Indians at Cleveland's Municipal Stadium. But the next night, before more than sixty-seven thousand fans, DiMaggio was shut down by the pitching of Al Smith and Jim Bagby, Jr., and two superb fielding plays by third baseman Ken Keltner. DiMaggio's stats for those 56 games: a .408 batting average fueled by 91 hits (56 singles, 16 doubles, 4 triples, 15 home runs); 55 runs batted in and 56 runs scored; 22 multiple-hit games. The Yanks were a fourth-place team on the day the streak began; they led the pack by 6 games when it ended.

Ted Williams was having a beaut of a season himself. Feasting on AL pitching, the Red Sox slugger fattened up his batting average to .39955

Dutch Treat Is Hard to Beat

....

Think about it: to break southpaw Johnny Vander Meer's single-season record, a pitcher would have to hurl three consecutive no-hitters. That's because "Vandy" fired back-to-back blankings on June 11 and June 15 of 1938. His victims on those respective dates were the Boston Bees and the Brooklyn Dodgers.

Cincinnati southpaw Johnny Vander Meer relied on his sinker and his fastball in hurling back-to-back no-hitters in mid-June 1938.

Yankees coach Art Fletcher (left) is joined in song by utility infielder Jerry Priddy (second from left), coach Earle Combs (third from left), short-stop Phil Rizzuto (center), third baseman Red Rolfe (fourth from right), right fielder Tommy Henrich (third from right), and first baseman Johnny Sturm (right) to celebrate their team's 1941 World Series victory over Brooklyn. Opposite: Joltin' Joe DiMaggio cracks a first-inning single against the Indians at Cleveland on July 16, 1941. It was the fifty-sixth consecutive game in which DiMaggio hit safely. The next night, the Indians' defense stopped him cold.

by the last day of the season. Rounded off, that comes to .400, and Boston skipper Joe Cronin offered to take Williams out of the lineup to preserve the kid's chance at becoming the first player in eleven years to reach the .400 mark. Williams declined the offer and, in a Sunday doubleheader in Philadelphia against the Athletics, he went 6-for-8 to wind up with a .406 batting average.

As satisfying as that season-long accomplishment was for him, Williams' self-proclaimed "most thrilling hit" came in that year's All Star Game at Detroit's Briggs Stadium on July 8. With the AL squad down 5–4 with 2 outs in the bottom of the ninth, Williams stunned the NL team when he socked a 3-run homer high into the right field stands to win the game, 7–5. The runner on first was none other than Joe DiMaggio.

The last baseball season before the country entered World War II was topped off by a Dodgers-Yankees World Series. The first 3 games were all 1-run squeakers, and the Dodgers led in the fourth game, 4–3. If Brooklyn could hold on, the Series would be tied at 2 games apiece.

With 2 outs and the bases empty in the top of the ninth, Tommy Henrich swung and missed the third strike. But the curveball of Dodgers reliever Hugh Casey eluded catcher Mickey Owen and Henrich made it to first before Owen could recover the ball and make a play. Given new life, the Yankees exploded for 4 unearned runs to win the game, and then beat the still-stunned Dodgers the next day to capture the World Series.

1942–1945: GREEN FIELDS GET THE GREEN LIGHT

The nation was abuzz with talk of the 1941 baseball season that had just ended: Joe DiMaggio's 56-game hitting streak, Ted Williams' successful run at hitting .400 for the season and game-winning home run in the All-Star Game, the tight NL pennant race between the Dodgers and the Cardinals that wasn't decided until late September, and the Yankees' come-from-behind victory in Game Four of the World Series that sparked their winning the Series outright the next day.

But excitement about the national pastime suddenly turned to anxiety about the international scene in the days and weeks following Japan's airborne attack on U.S. military installations at Pearl Harbor on the island of Oahu, Hawaii. The early-morning attack by 360 carrier-based Japanese planes on Sunday, December 7, resulted in the deaths of more than twenty-three hundred people, the destruction of two hundred U.S. planes and the destruction of, or heavy damage to, many key ships in the U.S. Pacific fleet.

In his address to Congress the next day, President Franklin Delano Roosevelt called December 7 "a date which will live in infamy." With nearly unanimous congressional support, the President signed the declaration of war that afternoon.

Rationing and bans on services, raw materials, and finished products in the civilian sector soon clouded the American way of life in a haze of doubt and confusion. The war effort was in full swing by early 1942, and virtually everything hinged on the progress of the war.

Would baseball continue? Should it continue? Could it continue? After all, the draft affected professional ballplayers—in both the majors and the minors—just as it did other civilians. Transportation was affected, not only in the rationing of new tires and the freeze on new sales, but in the ban on long trips by train or plane as well. Would the President and Washington lawmakers deem baseball a "nonpriority"?

Baseball Commissioner Kenesaw Mountain Landis wrote to President Roosevelt in January, asking him what baseball should do.

On January 15, Roosevelt responded with what has since been called the "green-light letter." In it, the President enthusiastically supported the continuance of professional baseball as a means of keeping morale high. He even expressed his hope that "night games can be extended because it gives an opportunity to the day shift to see a game occasionally."

Although Landis had the final say in the matter, more than a few historians believe that it was Clark Griffith, owner of the Washington Senators,

Opening Game april 14th 1941

who convinced Roosevelt that baseball should continue. Indeed, Griffith had strong ties to the White House, and to the President in particular. Regardless of who had the President's ear, the national pastime endured.

Some dismiss the game of that era, viewing player stats and the caliber of play with circum-spection. Certainly hundreds of ballplayers—including many stars—lost key years to military service, and the overall talent pool wasn't as strong as usual. But being able to follow big-league baseball during those years proved to be a welcome respite for the men and women serving in the armed forces and for their families back home.

Above, left: The photo was taken in 1943—years before big-league ballclubs started traveling by air. So why was this U.S. bomber flying low over Yankee Stadium? Perhaps it was piloted by a Yankees fan on his way overseas. **Above:** World War II had yet to draw the United States into direct military action, but patriotic fervor was in the air for the opening game of the 1941 season, as President Roosevelt shows his pitching form.

BIG-LEAGUE HIGHLIGHTS AT A GLANCE: 1942–1945

1942

Ted Williams wins the Triple Crown with a .356 batting average, 36 home runs, and 137 runs batted in, but the country's baseball writers select New York Yankee Joe Gordon as AL MVP.

Pitcher-turned-outfielder Stan Musial plays his first full season for the St. Louis Cardinals and hits .315 with 72 RBI. He goes on to post a .331 batting average with 475 home runs and nearly 2,000 RBI in a career that lasts through 1963.

The Cardinals defeat the Yankees in the World Series, 4 games to 1.

1943

World War II rages on many fronts and rubber is in short supply, so a new baseball is manufactured using balata, a rubberlike substance. Initial results are not good: a third of the games end in shutouts, and no home runs are hit until the twelfth game of the season. Unused baseballs from the 1942 season are brought out of retirement while manufacturers rush to produce a livelier baseball.

In the World Series, the Yankees beat the Cardinals by the same 4-games-to-1 margin the Cardinals enjoyed the previous fall.

Cardinals swifty Terry Moore serves up a plateful of dust to Yankees catcher Bill Dickey during the 1942 World Series.

1944

Baseball's first commissioner, Judge Kenesaw Mountain Landis, dies at the age of seventy-eight. The following spring, club owners elect Albert B. "Happy" Chandler, a U.S. senator from Kentucky, to succeed him.

Detroit Tigers lefty Hal Newhouser finally hits his stride, going 29–9 with a 2.22 ERA. The next year he goes 25-9 with a 1.81 ERA and wins 2 games in the World Series; he would stay on track in '46 with a 26–9 mark and a 1.94 ERA.

Not only are all this year's World Series games played in the same city, St. Louis, they're all played in the same venue: Sportsman's Park, the home of the Browns *and* the Cardinals. In their only World Series appearance, the Browns lose, 4 games to 2.

1945

U.S. government restrictions on wartime travel force the cancellation of the All-Star Game.

Pete Gray, twenty-eight, a one-armed outfielder who was sensational in the minors, hits .218 with 13 RBI for the third-place Browns.

The Tigers clinch the AL pennant on the last day of the season when Hank Greenberg blasts a grand slam homer to beat the Browns, 6–3. Greenberg had rejoined his team in midseason after a four-year stint in the Army.

The Chicago Cubs, in what would be their last postseason stint until 1984, lose a hard-fought World Series to the Tigers, 4 games to 3.

CHAPTER THREE

1946–1960: A Mad Dash, a Mays Catch, and a Maz Homer

Baseball, like the rest of America and the world, was in a state of flux after World War II. One of the more difficult tasks at hand was making room in the workforce for everyone who needed a job.

Returning veterans were itching to get back to their prewar lives in America's factories, farms, and offices, but in many instances their positions had been filled or eliminated while they were serving their country. Manpower on the home front during the early 1940s had been a precious commodity, now there was an overabundance of it.

Nowhere was that truer than in baseball. Even though teams were allowed to expand their twenty-five-man rosters to thirty in 1946, there were only so many positions available to the nearly four hundred big-league players returning from the service. Remember, there were only sixteen major league teams in existence at the time. Competition for big-league jobs was fierce. In time, things panned out, with some wartime players sticking around to have successful big-league careers alongside the era's marquee names.

Certainly racial integration in 1947 greatly improved the game. Following Jackie Robinson to the majors were such talents as Larry Doby, Roy Campanella, Dan Bankhead, Hank Thompson, and Monte Irvin in the 1940s, and Minnie Minoso, Vic Power, Sam Jethroe, Willie Mays, Ernie Banks, Hank Aaron, Curt Flood, and Frank Robinson in the 1950s. Their contributions to baseball's rich lore deserve every accolade they get. But baseball in the postwar years was also memorable because of exciting pennant chases and individual feats of skill that still echo through time.

Stan Musial races home with the Cardinals' third run of Game Six in the 1946 World Series. Enos Slaughter, whose single scored Musial from second, became the Series hero the next day when he dashed from first to home on a liner by Harry Walker and scored the winning run as the Cards edged the Boston Red Sox in 7 games.

Umpire Al Barlick and on-deck batter Marty Marion watch Enos Slaughter slide by Red Sox catcher Roy Partee for the go-ahead (and eventually game-winning) run in Game Seven of the 1946 World Series.

COUNTRY'S RUN

Baseball fans eagerly awaited the 1946 World Series to see what St. Louis Cardinal Stan Musial and Boston Red Sox Ted Williams would do.

Musial, in his fourth full big-league season, led the National League in batting average, slugging percentage, doubles, triples, runs, and hits. Williams, in his fifth season, hit .342 with 38 homers and 123 runs batted in.

The two men were unquestionably the stars of their respective ballclubs, but it was Musial's teammates who stole the spotlight and gave the Cardinals their third World Championship in five years.

The Series was deadlocked at 3 games apiece and the teams were tied at 3 runs apiece in Game Seven when the Cardinals came to bat in the bottom of the eighth. Enos "Country" Slaughter, an established star in his own right, singled to center.

That in itself was remarkable—he had suffered a broken elbow in Game Five when he was clipped by Boston starter Joe Dobson. It seemed you could take the boy out of the country but you couldn't take the "Country" out of the Series, because even after X-rays revealed a blood clot in Slaughter's right arm he convinced Cardinals skipper Eddie Dyer to leave him in the lineup. Country rewarded Dyer by hitting a run-scoring single in Game Six.

43

It was too long in coming, but major league baseball finally wised up and gradually but permanently reopened its doors to African-American ballplayers when Jackie Robinson took the field on April 15, 1947. Before the home game at Ebbets Field, Robinson was greeted by former U.S. Senator James Mead (left) and Brooklyn Borough President John Cashmore.

professional baseball was in its infancy, would have been pleased.

And though he went 0-for-3 against Braves pitching that day, Jackie keyed his team's come-from-behind victory. In the seventh, he laid down a sacrifice bunt to move Eddie Stanky into scoring position, with the heart of the Brooklyn lineup coming up.

In his rush to get the speedy Robinson at first, first baseman Earl Torgeson threw wildly. The ball caromed off Robinson and sailed into right field. Stanky took third and Robinson took second on the play. Pete Reiser then doubled them in to put the Dodgers on top to stay.

The twenty-eight-year-old Robinson went on to post a .297 batting average in his debut season. He stole a league-high 29 bases, scored 125 runs, and hit 31 doubles, 5 triples and 12 homers. For his efforts he was voted Rookie of the Year by the Baseball Writers' Association of America.

He accomplished all that despite encountering months of epithets, taunts, slurs, and physical threats from opposing players and their fans. He was spiked by base runners and thrown at by pitchers. Even before the season started, a few Dodgers informed club general manager and president Branch Rickey—the man responsible for signing Robinson in the first place—that they preferred not to play alongside a black man, and so they were traded to other teams.

A month into the 1947 season, Robinson was mired in a batting slump that his critics jumped on as proof that blacks couldn't cut it at the major league level. Robinson was, in the words of New York sportswriter Jimmy Cannon, "the loneliest man I have ever seen in sports."

But now it was the deciding game of the Series, and Slaughter, who was in great pain, was standing on first with no one out. However, Boston reliever Bob Klinger induced Whitey Kurowski to pop up and Del Rice to fly out.

Harry Walker then brought his .375 World Series batting average to the plate. When Dyer flashed the run-and-hit sign, Slaughter lit out for second. He was on his own if Walker elected not to swing, but Walker whacked Klinger's pitch over shortstop Johnny Pesky's head.

Leon Culberson scooped up the ball in center as Slaughter rounded second and ran for third. The partisan crowd of more than thirty-six thousand fans roared with anticipation as Slaughter blew by coach Mike Gonzalez's shouts and signs to stop at third base just as Pesky took Culberson's throw and turned clockwise to see where Walker was. Pesky then hurried his throw to home. It was too

late. Slaughter slid across the plate in a cloud of dust with the go-ahead run. Walker was credited with a double.

Boston got the first two men on in the top of the ninth, but Harry Brecheen quickly clamped down to win his third game of the Series and send Slaughter's "mad dash" into baseball history.

BREAKTHROUGH IN BROOKLYN

Jack Roosevelt Robinson was not the first black ballplayer to grace the majors, but he was the one who ultimately ripped down organized baseball's unofficial color line when he debuted with the Brooklyn Dodgers on April 15, 1947. Moses Fleetwood Walker, whose big-league debut preceded Robinson's by more than sixty years, when

Again with the New York Teams

• •

Past generations of baseball fans may have wondered if God had ordained that every World Series must include at least one team from New York City. Of the eighteen Fall Classics played from 1947 through 1964, sixteen featured at least one of the following representatives from the Big Apple: the Brooklyn Dodgers, the New York Giants, and the New York Yankees.

Pathfinder Jackie Robinson steals home in a game against the Boston Braves in late August 1948. Robinson's speed and daring on the base paths were two of many offensive weapons in his baseball arsenal.

But Jackie persevered. And once he began to turn things around, so did the Dodgers' fortunes turn. They went on to win the NL pennant by 5 games over the St. Louis Cardinals to earn the right to play the Yankees in the World Series.

Robinson played ten seasons in the big leagues, all with Brooklyn. He was instrumental in his team's successes during that time: six pennants and a World Championship. He hit .311 lifetime, was named the league's MVP for 1949, and was elected to the Hall of Fame in 1962. Twenty-five years later, Commissioner Peter Ueberroth announced that the Rookie of the Year Award—given to the best young player in each league—would be known as the Jackie Robinson Award.

The 1947 season was a tough but triumphant one for Robinson; it was a breakthrough season for baseball.

THE SHOT BY THE SCOT

The first-place Brooklyn Dodgers led the New York Giants by more than a dozen games as the dog days of summer wore on. It was mid-August, and the 1951 NL pennant race wasn't much of a race by then. Even many Giants fans seemed resigned to another Dodgers-Yankees World Series.

But Giants manager Leo Durocher rallied his troops. Beginning on August 12, they forged a 16-game winning streak that, combined with an ill-timed slump by the Dodgers, brought the Giants to within 7 games of first place by September 1. On that day and the next, the Giants beat the Dodgers to cut the lead to 5 games. But the Dodgers ran off 5 straight wins, including 1 against the Giants, to bounce back over the next week.

With ten days left in the season, the Dodgers still had a 4½-game lead. The Dodgers had 10 games remaining, the Giants 7. But when the dogfight ended and the dust had settled, the Dodgers had gone 4–6 and the Giants had won all 7 of their games. After waging a six-week battle that was nothing short of miraculous, the Giants had tied the Dodgers for the league's top spot. A 3-game playoff would decide the pennant.

The series opened on Monday, October 1, at the Dodgers' home park of Ebbets Field, the Giants winning, 3–1. The next day the visiting Dodgers returned the favor by pasting their hosts

Now comes the hard part: Bobby Thomson has just socked a Ralph Branca pitch into baseball immortality to give the Giants a shot at the Yankees in the 1951 World Series. But before he can celebrate with his teammates back in the clubhouse, he must run the gauntlet of crazed Giants fans who have poured onto the Polo Grounds playing field.

at the Polo Grounds, 10–0. The NL season was now down to 1 game on Wednesday afternoon.

More than thirty-four thousand fans returned to the Polo Grounds for the clincher. The skies were overcast, as was the outlook for the mostly biased Giants crowd with its team behind, 4–1, and down to their last 3 outs.

Alvin Dark led off the Giants' ninth with a single that found a hole between first and second. Don

Mueller punched another single through the right side of the infield, sending Dark to third. Dodger ace Don Newcombe got Monte Irvin to pop out to first baseman Gil Hodges. Whitey Lockman, a left-handed hitter, then slapped an opposite-field double that scored Dark and sent Mueller to third. But Mueller sprained his ankle sliding into the bag, and reserve outfielder Clint Hartung was sent in to run for him.

Praise be to Bobby! While Bobby Thomson completes his home run trot to give the New York Giants an electrifying come-from-behind playoff victory over archrival Brooklyn to capture the 1951 NL flag, Giants skipper Leo Durocher has to be helped off the ground by his jacketed second baseman, Eddie Stanky. (The feet in the upper left-hand corner are probably those of third base umpire Larry Goetz.)

ly yelled, "The Giants win the pennant!" as the ballpark erupted into a chaotic swirl of noise, paper, and jumping fans that climaxed with Thomson being carried off the field on the shoulders of his teammates.

"The home run didn't excite me," Durocher said, reflecting on the game years later. "I was shocked. I never expected it." Neither did the Dodgers and their fans.

OVER THE SHOULDER

Willie Mays always insisted that he made better catches than the one he made in Game One of the 1954 World Series. Still, it is the defensive play for which he is best remembered.

Mays put together a monster season to help his team reach the Fall Classic. His .345 batting average led the majors, and his National League–leading 13 triples went nicely with his 41 homers, 33 doubles, and 110 RBI.

Don Mueller was second on the team, with a .342 average, and he led the majors in hits with 212. Five other Giants besides Mays were in double figures in home runs. New York's pitching staff led the league in ERA and shutouts, sparked by southpaw Johnny Antonelli's 21–7 record, 2.29 ERA, and 6 shutouts.

The Giants' Series opponents were the Cleveland Indians. Along with the pitching of dual 23-game winners Bob Lemon and Early Wynn, 19-game winner Mike Garcia, a 15-win season from Art Houtteman, and thirty-five-year-old Bob

At this point, Dodgers manager Chuck Dressen lifted Newcombe for Ralph Branca, who had lost Game One on a 2-out, 2-run homer by the batter due up, Giants third baseman Bobby Thomson, nicknamed the "Staten Island Scot" because he was born in Glasgow but raised in Staten Island. It would be right-handed fastball pitcher against right-handed fastball hitter. Kneeling in the on-deck circle was Willie Mays.

Branca's first pitch was a fastball on the inside corner of the plate that Thomson took for a called strike. His second pitch, however, was a belt-high fastball, and Thomson connected. The line drive quickly rose over the infield and sailed for the stands. Left fielder Andy Pafko leaned helplessly against the wall as he looked up to see the ball disappear into the crowded bleachers. In the radio booth, announcer Russ Hodges repeated-

A Mad Dash, a Mays Catch, and a Maz Homer

Feller's 13–3 record, the Indians also boasted the league leaders in batting average (Bobby Avila, .341) and home runs and runs batted in (Larry Doby, with 32 and 126, respectively).

Game One in the cavernous Polo Grounds was knotted at 2–2 going into the top of the eighth. Leadoff batter Doby coaxed a walk off Giants starter Sal Maglie. Al Rosen singled. That was it for Maglie, and Don Liddle came on in relief. The first man he faced was Vic Wertz, who had already whacked a 2-run triple and 2 singles in the game. Wertz jumped on Liddle's first pitch and socked the ball so hard that in a heartbeat it was soaring high and deep into center field. Mays had played Wertz to pull.

But Mays saw the ball, turned, and raced to an area of the outfield just to the right of dead center. His head down, his back to the infield, and running full-out, Mays looked over his left shoulder and picked up the flight of the ball—now some four hundred fifty feet (137.1m) away from the plate. In full stride and a dozen feet (3.6m) from the high outfield wall, he reached up and caught the ball over his shoulder. As Mays whirled and threw to the cutoff man, his cap flew off and he fell to the ground.

His throw to second baseman Davey Williams was so good that Williams quickly fired the ball home to keep Doby from scoring. Rosen had to scurry back to first. Both runners were left stranded when the next two batters failed at the plate.

The teams were still locked in a 2–2 struggle when the Giants came to bat in the bottom of the tenth. Bob Lemon, still pitching for the Indians, got the first man out but walked Mays, who promptly stole second. Hank Thompson was intentionally walked to set up a double play situation.

Next up was pinch hitter James "Dusty" Rhodes, a .341 hitter during the regular season, and .333 off the bench. He lofted Lemon's first pitch into the right field seats for a two-hundred-sixty-foot (79.2m) home run to win the game, 5–2.

That's baseball for you. The game-saving catch was made on a ball that traveled some four hundred fifty feet (137.1m); the game-winning hit traveled little more than half that distance.

The Giants went on to sweep the Indians in 4 games. Rhodes went 4-for-6 with 2 homers and 7 RBI in the Series. And in baseball's rich lore, Mays' sparkling play in Game One is still known as "The Catch."

It is the most famous catch in postseason history: the Giants' Willie Mays makes an over-the-shoulder grab of Vic Wertz's booming drive in Game One of the 1954 World Series. No wonder ballplayer-turned-broadcaster Joe Garagiola spoke of Mays' glove as "the place where triples go to die."

JOHNNY ON THE SPOT

Yankees fans could gloat. Their team had bested the Brooklyn Dodgers in all five World Series matchups involving the two franchises. The cry from the Brooklyn faithful was always "Wait 'til next year."

So, when the two teams faced off in the 1955 Fall Classic, history was on New York's side. As in other years, they had strong pitching and solid hitting, powered, in part, by AL MVP Yogi Berra. The Dodgers countered with their own superb pitching staff and an awesome everyday lineup that led the majors in home runs and runs batted in. Berra's counterpart, Roy Campanella, was the NL MVP. Yankees slugger Mickey Mantle was hampered by a leg injury, and saw only limited action in the Series.

But in the end, it was the Dodgers' third starter who was the postseason hero and took home Series MVP honors.

Left-hander Johnny Podres, who had posted a disappointing 9–10 record with an ERA close to 4 during the regular season, had already won Game Three to put his team back in contention after the Yankees had won the first 2 contests. That seemed to rally the Dodgers, because they won the next 2 games to go ahead in the Series. But the Yankees came back to win Game Six behind Whitey Ford. The Series finale at Yankee Stadium pitted Podres against fellow lefty and Game Two winner Tommy Byrne.

Thanks to a run-scoring single and a sacrifice fly by first baseman Gil Hodges, the Dodgers led 2–0 going into the bottom of the sixth. Dodgers skipper Walt Alston had moved Jim Gilliam from left field to second base and replaced him in left with Sandy Amoros. Billy Martin coaxed a walk from Podres to start what the Yankees hoped was a rally. Gil McDougald then beat out a bunt just inside the third baseline. With the tying runs aboard, Berra, who was batting .455 for the Series, came to bat.

The Dodgers played the left-handed power hitter to pull the ball down the right field line, but Berra sliced the ball down the left field line. At the crack of the bat, both runners took off. But so did Amoros, who'd been shading Berra toward center. He raced toward the line and extended his gloved right hand as he applied the brakes to avoid hitting the wall. He snared the ball, turned, and fired it to cutoff man Pee Wee Reese, who whipped the ball across the infield to Hodges to double up McDougald at first. Podres then retired Hank Bauer on a groundout.

Dodgers fans heaved a sigh of relief when Podres worked out of a fix after the Yanks put runners on first and third with 1 out in the eighth. His team still clinging to that frail 2–0 lead in the bottom of the ninth, the twenty-two-year-old Podres had to face three very tough hitters in Bill Skowron, Bob Cerv, and Elston Howard. He induced Skowron to tap the ball back to him for out number 1. He got Cerv to hit a fly ball to Amoros for out number 2. When Podres made Howard hit a 6–3 (third to first) groundout to end the game and the Series, the man in the spotlight—and the man on the spot—had answered the prayers of Dodgers fans everywhere: next year was *now*.

YOGI'S EMBRACE

The Yankees avenged their 1955 World Series loss to the Dodgers by taking the 1956 Series in 7 games. But that particular Fall Classic is best remembered for one game—and one man.

In his first two seasons in the majors, Don Larsen had floundered with a foundering franchise, the St. Louis Browns–Baltimore Orioles, by going 7–12 with a 4.16 ERA and 3–21 with a 4.37 ERA. Larsen was part of a twofold, eighteen-player trade between the Orioles and the Yankees in late 1954. He turned things around with his new first-place team, going 9–2 in 1955 and 11–5 in the 1956. Each year his ERA was around 3.

Still, few observers would have predicted what he did in Game Five of the 1956 World Series, particularly after his shelling in Game Two.

Larsen's mound opponent that day was thirty-nine-year-old veteran Sal Maglie. Maglie's 13–5 record in a season-long pennant battle between the Dodgers, Milwaukee Braves, and Cincinnati Reds was highlighted by a no-hitter against the Phils

Dodgers pitchers such as Sandy Koufax and Don Drysdale still get more "ink," but it was Johnny Podres who hurled one of the franchise's biggest wins. Here is the form that brought the southpaw fame in the 1955 World Series.

down the stretch. And on this day against Larsen, Maglie was perfect through 3⅔ innings until Mickey Mantle socked a pitch that stayed just inside the right field foul pole to give the Yanks a 1–0 lead.

Larsen himself hadn't allowed a base runner through 5⅓.Then in the fifth, on a 2–2 count, Gil Hodges lined Larsen's 1-out pitch to deep left-center field. Mantle ran the ball down and made a superb one-handed catch to keep his teammate's effort intact.

By the seventh inning, the Yankees' lead was 2–0. But the big story was that Larsen was perfect after throwing 66 pitches. By the eighth he had thrown 74 pitches and was still perfect. And though a few Dodgers hitters put a charge into the ball, New York's defense was flawless.

Larsen's teammates steadfastly observed baseball's cherished superstition that one does not mention a no-hitter while it's in progress, so Mantle was horrified when, in their dugout, Larsen himself strolled over, lightly punched him in the arm, and said, "Look at the scoreboard, Mick. Two innings to go. Think I'll make it?"

Carl Furillo led off the Brooklyn ninth by fouling off 2 pitches, taking a ball high, and fouling off 2 more. He stroked Larsen's next pitch to right, where Hank Bauer caught the ball for the first out. The second batter was Roy Campanella, who slugged Larsen's first pitch deep but foul into the left field stands. Campy then hit a grounder to second baseman Billy Martin for out number 2.

Dale Mitchell was sent in to bat for Maglie. Mitchell, a left-handed contact hitter who averaged close to .430 as a pinch hitter for the Dodgers that year, took Larsen's first pitch for a ball outside. The second pitch was a called strike. Then a swing and a miss for strike 2. Larsen then threw a hanging curveball that Mitchell fouled off to the left.

Larsen fired a high fastball. Mitchell started to swing but held up. It didn't matter. Home plate umpire Babe Pinelli shot his right hand into the air for strike 3. The noise level at Yankee Stadium was deafening as catcher Yogi Berra rushed to his battery mate, leaped, and gave the hurler a bear hug. Don Larsen's ninety-seventh pitch seared his name into the record books.

Unhittable and unbelievable: catcher Yogi Berra is the first to reach his battery mate, Don Larsen, after Larsen put an exclamation point on his perfect game in the 1956 World Series by striking out Dale Mitchell. Four days earlier, Larsen had failed to last 2 innings against the Dodgers' powerhouse lineup.

MAZEROSKI'S NINTH SYMPHONY

The first time the New York Yankees met the Pittsburgh Pirates in the World Series was in 1927. The Yankees, with Babe Ruth, Lou Gehrig, Earle Combs, Tony Lazzeri, and Bob Meusel, swept the Pirates in 4 games, outscoring them 23 to 10.

The second time the two franchises met was in 1960. After 6 games the Yankees had outscored the Pirates 46 to 17 by winning Games Two, Three, and Six by the respective scores of 16–3, 10–0, and 12–0. But a win is a win, and the Pirates claimed Games One, Four, and Five by the respective scores of 6–4, 3–2, and 5–2. Going into the decisive Game Seven at Pittsburgh's Forbes Field, it was anybody's guess whether it would be a pitcher's duel or another blowout.

The Pirates scored 2 runs in the bottom of the first off Yankees starter Bob Turley and 2 more runs in the bottom of the second, 1 off Turley and 1 off reliever Bill Stafford.

Yanks first baseman Bill Skowron blasted a solo home run into the lower right field stands in the top of the fifth to make the score 4–1. In their next at bat, the Yankees mounted a comeback on Mickey Mantle's run-scoring single and a 3-run homer by Yogi Berra. In the top of the eighth, the Yankees added 2 more runs to make it a 7–4 New York lead.

The Pirates exploded for 5 runs in their half of the eighth to go ahead, 9–7. A crucial play came when, with a runner on first and no outs, Bill Virdon smashed a grounder that had "double play" dented into it. But the ball took a bad hop and struck Yankees shortstop Tony Kubek in the throat, sending him sprawling to the dirt and putting runners on first and second. After scoring a pair of single runs, the Pirates forged ahead on reserve catcher Hal Smith's 3-run homer.

New York scored a pair of runs in the top of the ninth to knot the score at 9–9. Ralph Terry, who got Don Hoak to fly out to end the Pirates' eighth-inning uprising, took the mound to start the bottom of the ninth. Normally a starter, Terry pitched into the seventh inning of Game Four, but lost a tough 3–2 decision. Now, four days later, with the Series on the line, he was being called on by manager Casey Stengel to be a reliever. As Game Seven unfolded—and perhaps not immedi-

The Pirates' Bill Mazerowski starts applying the brakes just as he is enveloped in a sea of teammates and fans at home plate. They're all going to celebrate Mazerowski's homer that gave Pittsburgh the 1960 world championship.

ately apparent to most observers then—-Stengel had had Terry warm up in the bullpen nearly every time the Yankees got into hot water. Terry was a gamer, but he was not fresh when he faced second baseman Bill Mazeroski to lead off the bottom of the ninth.

"Maz" had gotten 7 hits in the Series thus far, one of them a 2-run homer that was the Pirates' margin of victory in Game One. Game Seven was more than two and a half hours old when he

stepped to the plate. It was righty against righty. Mazeroski took Terry's first pitch for a ball.

Terry then threw a slider. But instead of arriving low in the strike zone, the pitch was letter high, and Mazeroski swung and connected. The ball sailed over the left field wall, and Pittsburgh could—for the first time in thirty-five years—claim bragging rights to being World Series champions.

1961-1981: Baseball Expands and Contracts

Major league baseball greatly expanded its geographical reach in the late 1950s when the Brooklyn Dodgers and the New York Giants moved to Los Angeles and San Francisco, respectively. But the total number of teams remained at sixteen—eight in each league.

That changed in 1961 with the addition of the Los Angeles Angels and the new Washington Senators (the original franchise had become the Minnesota Twins). The following year the National League also swelled to ten clubs with the New York Mets and the Houston Colt .45s. Several other franchises relocated and new ones were created clear into the late 1970s.

Other big changes during this period included the demise of the old reserve system, which had given clubs the right to reserve a player's services for the following year even if the player and the club had not agreed to the terms of a new contract; substantial increases in players' salaries, due in part to salary arbitration; work stoppages involving players as well as umpires; a tremendous increase in television coverage (and the introduction of night games in the World Series); and the establishment in 1965 of the free agent draft, which allowed clubs to draft negotiating rights to the nation's high school and college players.

But the on-field events of the period are what fans remember best.

If this isn't a classic home run swing, what is? Roger Maris creams a Tracy Stallard fastball into the right field stands of Yankee Stadium to break Babe Ruth's single-season home run mark. There is a nice symmetry to the phrase "61 in '61"—but the controversy surrounding the legitimacy of the record, combined with unceasing media attention, nearly crushed Maris in his historic pursuit.

Frenzied fans go after the record-breaking home run ball off the bat of Roger Maris. It happened in the fourth inning of a scoreless ballgame on Sunday, October 1, 1961. As this photo shows, one fan momentarily caught the ball in his suit jacket, but the ball rolled off the fabric and into the waiting hands of Brooklyn teenager Sal Durante. Maris' home run not only put the slugger into the record books, it also won the ballgame, 1–0.

THE BALL SAL DURANTE CAUGHT

Yankee Stadium was only a third full that warm Sunday afternoon, but Sal Durante was in the right field stands among a group of fans packed together like sardines. At about 2:45 P.M., a baseball whistled toward them. Another man tried to net the ball with his suit jacket, but the ball rolled off the fabric and Durante grabbed it. The Brooklyn teenager had caught the last ball Roger Maris hit in his home park in 1961.

And what a hit it was. Not only did it account for the only run of the game, it was the slugger's sixty-first home run of the year, breaking Babe Ruth's single-season mark by 1. Yet joy was not the emotion Maris felt as he rounded the bases, it was more a sense of relief that his ordeal was over.

That season Maris and teammate Mickey Mantle hit home runs at a pace that grabbed the attention of baseball fans everywhere. Although Mantle succumbed to illness in September, he still cracked 54 to Maris' 61, making them baseball's greatest single-season home run duo of all time.

Ruth hit his 60 homers in a 154-game season in 1927. Maris and Mantle were playing out their drama in a 162-game season. Therefore, declared Major League Baseball Commissioner Ford Frick in late July, a player would have to hit his sixty-first homer before his team's 155th complete game of the season in order to officially break Ruth's record. Some people applauded the ruling; others hated it.

Frick's ruling, coupled with the media's relentless pursuit of Maris as he drew closer to 61 homers, made the young slugger's life a daily grind. Cameras, microphones, and notepads were constantly shoved in his face, and the normally reserved Maris grew surly and sometimes combative with the people who kept asking him the same questions over and over.

So, after he socked Boston righty Tracy Stallard's 2–0 fastball into the right field stands, Maris "went blank" as he rounded the bases. Maris may have hit number 61 in the fourth inning of the Yanks' 162nd game of the year, but his teammates—especially Mantle—were elated for him. They pushed him out of their dugout to receive a standing ovation from the small but appreciative crowd that witnessed history in "the House that Ruth built."

Durante did not give the famous baseball to Maris. Instead, the ball went to California restaurateur Sam Gordon, who had offered a $5,000 reward to any fan who caught the ball and presented it to him. (Maris eventually got the ball, which later made its way to the National Baseball Hall of Fame and Museum in Cooperstown, New York.)

Maris did sock 1 more homer that year, and it won a ball game, too: against the Cincinnati Reds in Game Three of the World Series, which the Yankees won in 5 tilts.

THE FATHER'S DAY PERFECTO

It was only June 21, Father's Day, but the first-place Philadelphia Phillies were already feeling the heat of a pennant race. The NL race in 1964 was a dogfight, and they were looking to increase their meager lead over the Giants with a double-header sweep of the last-place New York Mets at Shea Stadium.

Veteran Jim Bunning was on the mound for the Phils for the first game. In the stands that afternoon were his wife, Mary, and the couple's oldest child, twelve-year-old Barbara, who had traveled from their home in Philly to support their favorite player and team. The perfect setting on a perfect afternoon.

Bunning took immediate control of the game. He had command of a nasty fastball and a good curve, but his slider was the pitch that baffled the Mets as the game moved along. Ron Hunt smashed a long drive to right field in the fourth, but the ball curved foul and Hunt was then retired.

In the fifth, left-handed hitter Jesse Gonder pulled a Bunning pitch that Phils second baseman Tony Taylor dived for and gloved. Still on his knees, Taylor threw to first baseman John Herrnstein for the out. It was the key play of the game.

The Phils tripled their 2–0 lead in the sixth—2 of their 4 runs coming on a double by Bunning. But it was the righty's pitching, not his hitting, that was the story. Through 7 innings, and then 8, Bunning was masterful. No one from the home team had reached base.

The Mets took their last shot at Bunning in the bottom of the ninth. Leadoff hitter Charlie Smith fouled out to Bobby Wine. George Altman struck out. John Stephenson, a left-handed batter, was sent in to pinch-hit. Stephenson never had a chance. Bunning struck him out too, and nailed down a perfect game before thirty-two thousand partisan Mets rooters.

A perfect performance and a total of 10 strikeouts. And by virtue of his no-hitter six years earlier with the Detroit Tigers, Bunning had become the first pitcher in big-league history to hurl a winning no-hitter in each league. The Phils won the second game too, increasing their lead over the Giants. And though they faltered down the stretch and lost the pennant to the Cardinals, the Phils could boast of having the NL Rookie of the Year in Dick Allen and a Father's Day "perfecto" from Jim Bunning.

PITCHING CLINIC AT CANDLESTICK

Boston's Carl Yastrzemski hit only .301 but won the AL batting title in 1968. There were 335 shutouts pitched in the majors that year. Batting averages plummeted. St. Louis Cardinal Bob Gibson crafted a 1.12 ERA to go with his 22–9 season, while Detroit Tiger Denny McLain became the first pitcher in thirty-four years to win at least 30 games. It clearly was the year of the pitcher.

At no point was this fact more evident than in a twenty-four-hour period at San Francisco's Candlestick Park in mid-September. On Tuesday night, September 17, the Giants opened a series against the Cardinals, who, two days earlier, had clinched their second consecutive NL championship. The Giants finished second.

There was nothing at stake for either team that night. Perhaps that is why fewer than ten thousand fans were on hand. Or perhaps it was because Gibson's 20 wins were up against Gaylord Perry's 14–14 mark. But one hour and forty minutes later, those fans were on their feet and cheering at the top of their lungs: Perry had pitched a 1–0 no-hit win. Ron Hunt's first-inning homer was the game's only tally.

Perry struck out nine, walked two, and allowed only 2 balls to be hit out of the infield. He recorded 12 groundouts, including 2 in the ninth off the bats of pinch hitters Lou Brock and Bobby Tolan. Perry then blew a called third strike past Curt Flood to end the game. The only threats to

On election day in 1994, Republican incumbent Jim Bunning got nearly 75 percent of the vote in Kentucky's fourth congressional district. But on Father's Day in 1964, veteran pitcher Jim Bunning got 100 percent of the twenty-seven Mets batters he faced in Shea Stadium. Here, Bunning wings another unhittable pitch plateward in his perfect game.

The 1968 season was all about pitching, as any encyclopedic stat book will show, and nowhere was that truer than at Candlestick Park in San Francisco on September 17 and 18. The Giants' Gaylord Perry fired a no-hitter against the Cardinals the first night, and on the following afternoon Cardinal Ray Washburn (pictured) returned the favor by hurling a no-hitter against the Giants.

Perry's bid for a no-hitter came in the sixth. Dal Maxvill slapped a bouncer up the middle that Perry snared and threw to first baseman Willie McCovey. Moments later the two reversed their roles, as McCovey made a fine stab of Tolan's 2-out smash and threw to Perry, covering the bag.

Ray Washburn didn't learn of Perry's no-hitter until the next morning at the hotel where the Cardinals were staying. (Because Sunday's pennant-clincher was followed by a day off on Monday, the right-hander was permitted to fly home to see family.) Now it was his turn to pitch.

Only four thousand seven hundred fans attended the Wednesday afternoon tilt, but it was a doozy. Washburn and Giants starter Bob Bolin were locked in a scoreless duel through six. But in the Cardinals' seventh, Orlando Cepeda singled, went to second on a force play, and scored on Mike Shannon's double. The Cardinals added another run later in the game to make the score 2–0.

But Washburn was the man of the hour. He got out of a 2-out jam in the first by striking out Dick Dietz with runners in scoring position. A bit wild with his fastball and sinker over the course of the game, Washburn had run the count to 3–2 on several batters and walked five. But through 8 innings, he'd not given up a single hit.

Washburn gutted it out in the ninth against sluggers Willie Mays and McCovey, and when he induced McCovey to lift a soft liner to Flood in center, Washburn had recorded his own no-hitter—the second hitless victory pitched at Candlestick in less than twenty-four hours.

METS MUFFLE THE SONGBIRDS

Don Buford pasted Tom Seaver's second pitch of the ball game over the right field fence. Not only did that give the Baltimore Orioles an early lead in Game One of the 1969 World Series, it sent a message to the New York Mets and their fans that it would take another miracle for them to win the championship.

The "Miracle Mets" of '69 got their moniker because they overcame a 9½-game deficit in August to win the NL Eastern Division, and then swept the highly favored Atlanta Braves in the first-ever NL Championship Series. The Mets, an expansion team in 1962, never placed higher than seventh during a regular season. For them to

Tom Seaver's nickname was "Tom Terrific," and with a lifetime win-loss record of 311–205, it's easy to see why. Seaver was part of a supertalented Mets pitching staff in the late 1960s and early 1970s. His 25–7 record in 1969 was a big reason why the overachieving Mets were baseball's best team that year.

There's a Whiff of Tiger in the Air

·····························

The Detroit Tigers made a dramatic comeback to beat the St. Louis Cardinals in the 1968 World Series, but Game One is what many fans still remember best. Cardinals ace Bob Gibson sat down seventeen Tigers in 9 innings of 5-hit shutout work. He whiffed seven of the first nine Detroit batters he faced, and capped off his masterful performance by blanking the last three in the ninth. Gibby's 17 strikeouts are a World Series record.

This composite photo from the 1968 World Series shows power pitcher Bob Gibson in his prime.

the Orioles got, and the Mets rallied in the bottom of the tenth to win, 2–1, on a throwing error by reliever Pete Richert.

Baltimore hitters popped 2 homers in the third inning of Game Five to take a 3–0 lead. The Mets got 2 of those runs back in their half of the sixth when Donn Clendenon socked a 2-run homer to left. The base runner, Cleon Jones, had been struck on the foot by a pitch that the Orioles argued had hit the dirt around home plate. Jones claimed the shoe polish on the ball proved he had been hit, and home plate umpire Lou DiMuro agreed.

Light-hitting Al Weis homered in the Mets' seventh to tie the score. In the eighth, the Mets—aided by a pair of Baltimore infield errors—put 2 on the board and held on to win the game, 5–3.

The Amazing Mets. The Miracle Mets. The World Champion Mets.

BROOKSIE WHIRLS AND THROWS

Third baseman Brooks Robinson used what he calls a medium-sized Rawlings glove during his lifelong career with the Baltimore Orioles.

It might as well have been a Hoover upright.

Seemingly all smoked liners, bad-hop bouncers, and line-hugging dribblers were destined to be sucked up into that glove of his for an out or an assist. Brooksie won sixteen consecutive Gold Glove awards and set an AL record for third basemen when he was tops in fielding percentage for ten straight seasons. He set career records—some of which still stand—for putouts, assists, fielding percentage, and double plays turned.

He was a fine hitter during his prime, winning the league's MVP Award in 1964 with a .317 batting average and a league-leading 118 runs batted in. He smashed 268 homers and knocked in more than 1,300 runs in twenty-three regular seasons.

Baseball fans who didn't get to see Robinson play on an everyday basis knew him best for his postseason performances, particularly in the 1970 World Series. Not only did he hit .429 with 2 homers, 2 doubles, and 6 RBI for the five games, he fielded spectacularly well. Highlights included:

Game One. With the score tied at 3 apiece in the sixth, Cincinnati Red Lee May blasted a shot

contend for, much less win, their division and the pennant in only their eighth year, was indeed amazing. And, on paper at least, the Orioles were the better team when the World Series opened on October 11 in Baltimore.

As it turned out, the Mets failed to pull off another miracle to win Game One, but the rest of the Fall Classic was something else.

In Game Two, Mets starter Jerry Koosman had a no-hitter through 6 innings. The Orioles finally broke through in the seventh on a single, a stolen base, and another single. Those were the only 2 hits Koosman gave up, and his team rallied in the top of the ninth to win, 2–1.

Back in New York's Shea Stadium for Game Three after a travel day, the Mets jumped out to an early lead off Orioles starter Jim Palmer and never looked back. But the 5–0 blanking is best remembered for the glove work of Mets center fielder Tommy Agee.

Down 3–0, the Orioles mounted a rally in their half of the fourth by putting runners on first and third with 2 outs. Elrod Hendricks hit a Gary Gentry pitch to deep left-center, but Agee was on his horse at the crack of the bat and made a nifty backhanded catch on the warning track.

The Orioles threatened again in the seventh. With 2 outs and the bases loaded, Nolan Ryan was brought in to face Paul Blair. Blair jumped on a pitch and sent a sinking liner into right-center. Again, Agee ran full tilt, this time making a one-handed grab of the ball while he slid on his belly.

The Mets' magic in the outfield prevailed in Game Four as well. With 1 out and runners on first and third in the top of the ninth, Oriole Brooks Robinson hit what at first looked to be a gapper that would go for extra bases and score both runners. But right fielder Ron Swoboda ran hard, dived, and made a sparkling one-handed catch. The sacrifice fly scored the tying run, but that's all down the line that was backhanded by Robinson, who then spun around and fired to first for the out. A seventh inning homer by Brooksie gave the Orioles a 4–3 win.

Game Two. Threatening to add to their 4–0 lead, the Reds had a man on base with 1 out in the third. May again hit a hard one and Robinson again backhanded it, this time turning the smash into a "5-4-3" double play. The Orioles rallied to take the game, 6–5.

Game Three. Robinson killed potential rallies by turning a double play in the first, fielding a slow roller down the line in the second, and snaring a liner in the sixth.

Game Four. In a losing cause, Robinson went 4-for-4 at the plate, including a solo homer and a run-scoring single.

Game Five. Robinson dived to his left and snared Johnny Bench's low liner for the first out of the ninth. Two batters later he cleanly handled pinch hitter Pat Corrales' grounder and flipped to first for the out; it wasn't spectacular, but it ended the game and the Series.

The Orioles won four pennants (1966 and 1969–1971) and two World Series (1966 and 1970) with Robinson. His range, soft hands, quick reflexes, and accurate arm set the standard. And Brooksie could hit a little bit, too.

HISTORY ARRIVES ON THE SEVEN FIFTEEN

Hank Aaron was a survivor. His entire life up to the spring of 1974 was dotted by racial slurs, epithets, taunts, and slights, and for many months past he had endured hate mail, brutish fan behavior, and not always sympathetic media types while he forged ahead in breaking what for decades had been sacrosanct: Babe Ruth's career record of 714 regular-season home runs.

Aaron was forty years old at the start of the 1974 big-league season, his twenty-first. With the exception of his rookie year in 1954, he had never hit fewer than 24 home runs in a single season.

Baseball wisdom says that pitching and defense win games. If so, then 20-game winners Mike Cuellar, Dave McNally, and Jim Palmer provided the former while this man—third baseman Brooks Robinson—provided much of the latter. Robinson and the 1970 Orioles won their division by 15 games, swept the Twins in the playoffs, and disposed of the Reds in 5 games in the World Series.

Such consistency earned him the title of "Hammerin' Hank" and set the stage for his two most famous clouts.

The Atlanta Braves opened the '74 season against the Reds in Cincinnati. A capacity crowd of more than fifty-two thousand fans packed into Riverfront Stadium on April 4, hoping to see history made. Aaron needed only 1 homer to tie Ruth's record and 2 homers to send it crumbling.

Braves owner Bill Bartholomay had indicated before the season even began that he wanted his slugger to make history in front of the home folks in Atlanta, but Commissioner Bowie Kuhn vetoed that idea by telling Braves manager Eddie Mathews that Aaron should play in at least 2 of the 3 games at Cincy. The Braves complied, and on his first official hit of the season, Aaron drilled a 3–1 pitch off Reds starter Jack Billingham into the left-center field bleachers for a 3-run homer. Babe Ruth now had company at the top.

Aaron was not inserted into the lineup the next day, and went hitless in the third and final game of the Reds series. The odds were in his favor that he would set the record in Atlanta after all. After a travel day, the Braves were back at Atlanta–Fulton County Stadium for their home opener with the Dodgers. Nearly fifty-four thousand excited fans crammed into the ballpark, which, on the night of April 8, was a real media circus. In addition to the millions of radio listeners nationwide, there were an estimated thirty million viewers glued to their television sets at home.

Veteran southpaw Al Downing was on the mound for the Los Angeles Dodgers. He gave up a walk to Aaron in the second inning, and Aaron eventually came around to score the Braves' first run. The Dodgers scored 3 runs of their own in the top of the third, but in the bottom of the inning, with 2 outs and Darrell Evans on first because of an infield error, "Hammerin' Hank" stepped to the plate once again with a chance to tie the game and set the all-time home run record with one swing of his bat.

Downing's first pitch was a change-up in the dirt. Aaron waited patiently while that ball was thrown out and replaced with a new one that Downing rubbed up. Catcher Joe Ferguson gave the sign. At 9:07 P.M., Downing fired a low, hard slider that got too much of the plate, and Aaron belted it into the Georgia night. The ball soared over the left field fence and into the Braves'

Steady, heady, and ready—that was Hank Aaron. Baseball's all-time home run king averaged .305 at the plate with 33 homers and 100 RBI a season. In fact, he walloped 40 home runs at the age of thirty-nine. He was also a smart ballplayer, possessed a good glove and strong arm, and met his greatest challenge—the media pressure and hate mail as he was closing in on Babe Ruth's career homer mark—with grace and courage.

bullpen, where relief pitcher Tom House caught the ball on the fly.

As baseball's new home run king circled the bases, a few fans ran onto the field, fireworks exploded, cheers grew so loud that the noise sounded like a jet engine, and Aaron's teammates mobbed him at home plate. Oh, yes, and the Braves went on to win the game, 7–4.

BODY ENGLISH

Millions of people watching Game Six of the 1975 World Series must have thought Tony Kubek was psychic. The NBC broadcaster had just said that Boston Red Sox rookie Fred Lynn viewed the recent three-day rain delay as a plus because "he's been in a little bit of a slump. He's had time to go under the stands in center field and take a lot of extra hitting practice, trying to get back in the groove."

On the very next pitch, Lynn socked a 3-run homer to deep right field to put Boston up 3–0 over the Cincinnati Reds.

It stayed that way until the Reds tied the score in the top of the fifth. The big blow was Ken Griffey's 2-run triple to left-center field. Lynn raced to the warning track and leaped for the ball, which sailed just beyond his glove, caromed off the concrete wall and into right field, where Dwight Evans picked it up and fired it to the cut-off man. Time was called as soon as the play ended. Fenway Park was eerily silent, and all eyes turned to center field.

Lynn was lying in a heap at the base of the wall. Knowing his momentum would carry him crashing face-first into the concrete wall, he managed to spin himself around and, with his right foot, tried to push off the wall to lessen the impact. But his wet cleats slipped on the concrete surface and his tailbone and back smashed hard against the wall.

In a heartbeat, Evans, left fielder Carl Yastrzemski, trainer Charlie Moss, and manager Darrell Johnson were attending to their fallen teammate. Pitching coach Stan Williams soon joined them. Several minutes passed before they helped the dazed Lynn to his feet and the crowd could exhale. Moments later, as play resumed, Johnny Bench's long single easily scored Griffey from third to make it 3–3.

The Reds pulled ahead in the seventh. George Foster's 2-out double high off the center field wall scored Griffey and Joe Morgan, whose back-to-back singles led off the inning. The Reds added another run in the eighth when Cesar Geronimo lofted starter Luis Tiant's first pitch high and deep down the right field line for a home run. Roger Moret then relieved Tiant, who received a standing ovation from the Fenway faithful. Moret stopped the bleeding by coaxing 3 straight outs from the Reds.

Leading 6–3 going into the eighth, Cincinnati was only 6 outs away from the franchise's first World Championship in thirty-five years. But Lynn greeted Reds reliever Pedro Borbon by smashing a single off his leg. Borbon then walked Rico Petrocelli, and Reds skipper Sparky Anderson called on Rawly Eastwick to face Evans, who had homered off him in Game Three.

Eastwick outdueled Evans this time, fanning him on a 3–2 pitch well out of the strike zone. Rick Burleson then lined to Foster in short left for the second out.

Pinch hitter Bernie Carbo was up next for the Red Sox. Carbo, who cracked a pinch hit solo homer in Game Three, had been, coincidentally, the Reds' number one draft choice some ten years earlier.

Carbo took Eastwick's first offering right down the middle for a called strike. The next 2 pitches were balls. Carbo then swung at and missed an Eastwick fastball for strike 2. Carbo, protecting the plate, fouled off two more pitches before broadcaster Joe Garagiola got to make this call: "Deep center field—way back—way back—we're tied up!"

His arms out at his sides as he rounded third base and headed toward home, Carbo seemed to

Shown here in action against the Boston Red Sox during the 1975 World Series, the Reds' Tony Perez hit only .179 for the Series, but when he did connect, it helped his team's cause. Of his 5 hits, 3 were home runs (tops in the 7-game duel), and his 7 runs batted in were also the most of any batter in the Series.

Boston's Carlton Fisk watches the ball that he just whacked sail just fair of the left field foul pole for a home run to win Game Six of the 1975 World Series. Although the Cincinnati Reds won Game Seven—and the championship—the next night, for many fans it is Fisk's dramatic homer in the bottom of the twelfth inning of Game Six that is the legacy of the '75 Series.

be flying—emotionally and physically. He stayed in the game, taking over in left for Yastrzemski, who moved to first base.

The Reds went down one-two-three in their half of the ninth. Boston loaded the bases in the bottom of the inning on a Yastrzemski single sandwiched in between walks to Denny Doyle and Carlton Fisk.

For a moment it appeared that Lynn would be the hero of the game. He poked Will McEnaney's first pitch to the opposite field. Foster raced toward the left field line and made a very tough catch close to the wall. With no time to really plant himself, Foster slung the ball to Bench at the plate. The ball bounced once before Bench grabbed it with his mitt, whirled to his left, and made a swipe tag on Doyle's shoulder just as Doyle dived for the plate. It was a game-saving double play. Petrocelli then grounded to third to end the Boston threat.

Cincinnati almost scored in the tenth, but Dave Concepcion was left stranded at second.

Pete Rose led off the Reds' eleventh. After getting ahead of Rose, 1–2, reliever Dick Drago came inside with a pitch that home plate umpire Satch Davidson ruled had whisked Rose's shirt-sleeve. Rose was gunned down at second, though, when Fisk jumped out of his catcher's crouch, pounced on Griffey's bunt down the third base-line, and winged the ball to Burleson for the force-out.

With 1 down and Griffey on first, Morgan, who'd been limited to 5 hits in the Series, whacked Drago's 1–1 pitch to deep right field. Evans bolted for the warning track and, at the top of his leap, made a one-handed catch in front of the stands. He spun around and fired the ball to first to double up Griffey, who had made it all the way to third. Evans' throw was way wide of the bag, but Yaz fielded the ball cleanly in foul territory and flipped it to Doyle covering the bag for the second heart-stopping double play of the game.

Cincinnati put runners on first and second in the top of the twelfth, but reliever Rick Wise worked out of his self-made jam; Concepcion flied to Evans in right and Geronimo struck out looking.

Since entering the game in the tenth, Reds reliever Pat Darcy had retired all six batters he faced. More than thirty-five thousand Sox fans were restless.

Fisk led off for Boston in the bottom of the twelfth. Darcy's first pitch was high, ball 1. But Darcy's second pitch was knee high, and Fisk got his arms fully extended as he crushed the ball down the left field line. He knew that the ball was curling foul, so in a moment of pure boyish enthusiasm and hope he jumped into the air, waved his arms, and applied some body English to keep the ball in fair territory. Play-by-play announcer Dick Stockton's voice rose in anticipation as the ball rose in the night sky over Fenway: "There it goes! A long drive—if it stays fair—home run!"

The ball hit off the left field foul pole so high that many observers—Stockton included—initially thought the ball had gone over Fenway's famed Green Monster and into the net.

Rounding third and trotting the final ninety feet (27.4m) to home, Fisk had to elbow his way through delirious fans who had jumped onto the field to swarm their hero. It was pandemonium at the plate. Fisk's teammates, along with several fans, security guards and park attendants, and home plate umpire Satch Davidson, were all there when Fisk jumped onto the pentagonal rubber slab to make it official: Boston 7, Cincinnati 6.

And though the Cincinnati Reds bounced back to win the seventh and deciding game of the 1975 World Series, it is Game Six that best exemplifies one definition of "classic": a work of enduring excellence.

THE PRIME OF MR. OCTOBER

Free agent Reggie Jackson was looked on as an interloper when he signed with the New York Yankees prior to the 1977 season.

His meaty new contract, combined with his self-assured (some said cocky) style of play, created a hostile atmosphere as early as spring training. Several members of the New York press corps quickly prejudged him. During the season, many die-hard Yankees rooters booed him lustily when his name was announced over the PA system. Even Jackson's teammates—particularly after he was quoted in the June issue of *Sport* magazine as saying, "I'm the straw that stirs the drink"—scorned him.

His stormy relationship with Yankees skipper Billy Martin made things worse. Martin often jug-

They named a candy bar after him, you know. Perhaps that's because Reggie Jackson understood the concept of "the sweet spot." Here, the player knighted as "Mr. October" demonstrates what happens when the sweet spot of the bat meets a Burt Hooton offering in the 1977 World Series.

Reggie Jackson hits the first of his 5 home runs in the 1977 World Series. This one came off reliever Rick Rhoden in the sixth inning of Game Four.

It's 105 and counting. St. Louis speedster Lou Brock breaks Maury Wills' single-season mark of 104 stolen bases on September 10, 1974. Brock ended the season with 118 steals.

gled his lineup and had Jackson—normally a cleanup hitter—bat as low as sixth. And their blowup in the dugout during a nationally televised game in June crystallized for many the perception that dissension would cause this ballclub to self-destruct.

But the Yankees didn't self-destruct. They thrived. And Jackson, straw or not, certainly was a key ingredient in the Yankees' mix; he ended the season sporting a .286 batting average, a team-leading 110 runs batted in, 32 homers, 39 doubles, and 93 runs scored. The Yankees outlasted the Baltimore Orioles and the Boston Red Sox to win the AL East, then edged the Kansas City Royals in the playoffs to capture the pennant and face the Los Angeles Dodgers in the World Series.

Through the first four games, the Yankees led the Dodgers, 3–1. In Game Five, which the

Dodgers won by a score of 10–4, Jackson socked a home run in his last at bat: 1 pitch, one swing, 1 home run.

Game Six was played in front of a keyed-up crowd of fifty-six thousand noisy New Yorkers on a cool Tuesday evening at Yankee Stadium. A 2-run triple by first baseman Steve Garvey gave Los Angeles an early lead in the game. But in his first at bat Jackson drew a walk off Dodgers starter Burt Hooton and scored on Chris Chambliss' game-tying home run. The Dodgers countered with a third-inning solo shot off the bat of Jackson's namesake, Reggie Smith, to regain the lead, 3–2.

Thurman Munson led off the home half of the fourth with a single to left. Jackson lined Hooton's first pitch to him into the right field stands to put the Yanks back on top, 4–3. Hooton was quickly

pulled for reliever Elias Sosa, who gave up another run before getting out of the inning.

In the fifth, Jackson came to bat with 2 out and a man on first. He jumped on Sosa's first pitch and sent it into the right field stands for his second homer of the night. A 7–3 Yankee lead going into the bottom of the eighth brought the World Series crown closer. But Jackson wasn't done.

The oft-maligned slugger waited out Charlie Hough's first pitch, a dancing knuckler, and pasted it high and deep into the center field bleachers for his third straight home run of the game. Three pitchers, 3 pitches, three swings, 3 home runs. The place erupted.

Babe Ruth twice socked 3 homers in a World Series game, but never on just 3 pitches. Counting his Game Five clout, Jackson hit 4 homers on four pitches, and his homer in Game Four gave him a total of 5 for the Series—a new record. Jackson "touched 'em all" in the '78 and '81 World Series as well, but it is his awesome display of power in the 1977 Fall Classic that really earned him the nickname of "Mr. October."

TWO MONTHS' MISERY

Despite southpaw Fernando Valenzuela winning Rookie of the Year honors, despite Pete Rose breaking Stan Musial's NL record for career hits, despite the exciting brand of baseball played by the Oakland A's, despite a fifth no-hitter by Nolan Ryan, the 1981 season is best remembered for a players' strike that began in mid-June and lasted more than seven weeks.

The Major League Baseball Players Association voted for the strike, but only after team owners forced the group's hand by demanding a change in the system of compensation to teams losing key players to free agency. Simply put, the players refused to cough up what they had fought so hard to get in earlier bargaining sessions in the 1970s. Labor negotiations dragged on, ending only when the owners' strike insurance ran out.

More than seven hundred games were lost to the strike. Nearly $100 million was lost in player salaries and revenues from ticket sales, broadcast rights, and ballpark concessions. And then, in a misguided effort to generate fan interest—and add some much-needed capital—a "split season" was created. Teams leading their divisions before the strike were declared first-half winners. They would play the second-half divisional winners to determine which teams would play in the two league championship series. The Cincinnati Reds forged the best overall record in the NL Western Division but failed to make the playoffs because they didn't wind up with the best record for either half. The same fate befell the St. Louis Cardinals in the NL Eastern Division.

The season of strife and strike ended on the night of October 28. The Dodgers whipped the Yankees 9–2 in the sixth and decisive game of the World Series. Few in Cincinnati or St. Louis cared.

Don't tell Steve Howe, Steve Yeager, and Steve Garvey that 1981 was a bad year for baseball. They and their fellow Dodgers have just won the World Series over the Yankees. (And just for the record, not everyone on that Dodgers squad was named Steve.)

1982-1995: Learning to Fly

With the ugliness of the strike-shortened 1981 season still in the mirror, major league baseball wanted to put on its best face in 1982.

It did so with tight races in all four divisions. In fact, three of the four divisions weren't decided until the final weekend of the season. Only the St. Louis Cardinals, who were deprived of a shot at postseason glory the previous autumn because of the split-season arrangement, clinched earlier, but their NL Eastern Division crown still came as late as September 27.

The 1982 campaign presaged the good things to come for the next decade. Tight divisional races, nip-and-tuck playoffs to decide the pennant winners, thrilling World Series marked by wild comebacks, and the emergence of many of the game's biggest stars helped fill the stands like no other period in baseball history. And though the national pastime came crashing to the ground after a ruinous season-ending strike in 1994, Oriole Cal Ripken, Jr.'s record-setting night in Baltimore late in the 1995 season offered hope

that baseball would reclaim its hold on the American psyche.

HARVEY'S WALLBANGERS

In bartending parlance, a Harvey Wallbanger is a mixed drink that, if taken in excess, can quickly wreak havoc on one's faculties.

In baseball parlance, Harvey's Wallbangers were the sluggers on manager Harvey Kuenn's

A few years before he made a sparkling catch as a center fielder to preserve Juan Nieves' no-hitter in 1987, Robin Yount was a reliable shortstop for the Milwaukee Brewers. Here, Yount is the pivot man in a Brewers double play.

1982 Milwaukee Brewers, who could quickly wreak havoc on one's earned run average.

The squad featured six everyday players and one part-time player in double figures in home runs. In fact, the team as a whole reached the American League's walls and fences 216 times during the regular season. Four of those six every-day sluggers also knocked in more than 100 runs for the season.

Harvey's Wallbangers led the majors in RBI (843), runs scored (891), and slugging percentage (.455), while three of his stars were tops in the majors that year: AL MVP Robin Yount led in hits (210) and doubles (46), Paul Molitor in runs scored (136), and Gorman Thomas in home runs (39). The Brewers didn't just beat their opponents, they beat them up.

Milwaukee pitching was adequate enough to outduel the Baltimore Orioles on the last day of the season to capture the AL Eastern Division by a game and overtake the California Angels in the best-of-five championship series.

But in the World Series, even Brewer bats could not compensate for tired arms on the mound and the absence of ace reliever Rollie Fingers due to a torn muscle in September. So, despite being blanked 10–0 in Game One, the Cardinals went on to outhit and outpitch the Brewers to capture the Series in 7 games.

But in the beer capital of Milwaukee, Harvey's Wallbangers remained the toast of the town.

BRETT'S BAT

Brinkmanship is defined as "the art or practice of pushing a dangerous situation to the limit of safety before stopping."

For Joe Brinkman, the words "George Brett" might have been added after "stopping." Brinkman, crew chief of the four umpires officiating a 1983 midsummer game between the Kansas City Royals and the hometown Yankees, was only doing his job and following the official rules of baseball.

He upheld the out call that home plate umpire Tim McClelland signaled against Brett, the Royals' clutch-hitting slugger who moments earlier had socked a 2-out, 2-run, ninth-inning homer

An ump's gotta do what an ump's gotta do. In this instance that means restraining George Brett, who, as you can see from his serene facial expression and relaxed demeanor, only wishes to let home plate umpire Tim McClelland (not shown) know that he disagrees with the call.

off reliever Goose Gossage that gave the Royals a 5–4 lead.

After Brett stepped on home plate and trotted toward the excited, happy faces in the Royals' dugout, Yankees skipper Billy Martin sprang from the Yankees' dugout and told McClelland that the pine tar on Brett's bat handle was above the legal limit of eighteen inches (45.7cm) from the knob up. That is an infraction of the rules, Martin argued, and the batter must be called out.

McClelland and Brinkman measured the bat against the width of the plate, which is seventeen inches (43.1cm), and found that the goo on Brett's bat indeed ran well over the limit. McClelland called Brett out, in effect ending the game on a home run in the visitors' last at bat. Brett exploded off the bench and lit out for McClelland.

Coaches, players, and three umpires, including Brinkman, nearly gang-tackled the screaming Brett to keep him from assaulting McClelland, who, at six feet six inches (2.1m) and two hundred fifty pounds (113.5kg), stood firm and calm, mask in hand.

Later that day, the Royals lodged a protest with AL president Lee MacPhail. MacPhail reviewed the videotape of what would be called "the pine tar incident" and several days later announced that he was upholding the Royals' protest. MacPhail said that although the umpires' decision was "technically defensible"—meaning that McClelland and Brinkman were right—it wasn't in accord with the intent or the spirit of the rule to make that call. The umpires should have tossed out the bat, MacPhail said, but since they didn't Brett should not have been called out as a result of the umpires' interpretation of the rules.

The upshot of MacPhail's ruling was that the July 25 game was "suspended" from the point after which Brett had hit his home run. The game was resumed on August 18.

It didn't live up to its hype. One Royal in the top of the ninth and three consecutive Yankees in the bottom of the ninth made outs. Final score: Royals 5, Yankees 4. The Goose was cooked and the chaw of tobacco that Brett choked on during his tirade was at last digesting.

Before the 1984 season, baseball's playing rules committee amended what Billy Martin himself called "a lousy rule."

A little-known irony of the pine tar incident is that just two weeks earlier, virtually the same umpiring crew had discussed the rule in their locker room. The foursome was firm: too much pine tar, too bad; the man's out.

So much for empowering the umpires to make the right call.

CLARK'S CLOUT

The St. Louis Cardinals dropped the first 2 games of the 1985 NL Championship to the hometown Los Angeles Dodgers by scores of 4–1 and 8–2. Heading back to St. Louis, the Cardinals were counting on 18-game winner Danny Cox to stop the bleeding. Cox did, limiting the Dodgers to 2 runs on 4 hits in 6 innings of work while the highly touted speed of the Cardinals sparked a pair of rallies.

But disaster struck the team during pregame workouts the next day. Rookie Vince Coleman was injured when the automatic tarp machine was accidentally switched on as Coleman was trotting past it. The tarp rolled over Coleman's left leg and sidelined him with a bone chip.

Cardinals utility man Tito Landrum met the challenge, going 4-for-5 with 3 runs batted in as the Cardinals routed the Dodgers 12–2 and tied the series at 2 games apiece.

Game Five contrasted sharply with the previous day's barrage. Willie McGee and Ozzie Smith led off the game with walks, and third-place hitter Tommy Herr doubled his mates in. But Dodgers starter Fernando Valenzuela then settled down and kept the Cardinals scoreless over the next 7 innings. Meanwhile, the Dodgers tied the score in their half of the fourth when Ken Landreaux singled and Bill Madlock homered. It stayed 2–2 through the top of the ninth inning.

Dodgers manager Tommy Lasorda called on relief ace Tom Niedenfuer to pitch the ninth. After getting McGee to hit a foul pop-up near

Opposite: You can be sure that Dodgers manager Tommy Lasorda is about to reach for the antacid: Jack Clark jacks a Tom Niedenfuer pitch over the left field wall for a 3-run homer to give the Cardinals the 1985 NL pennant. Above: Jack Clark and Vince Coleman are joyous over Clark's game-winning and pennant-clinching home run against the Los Angeles Dodgers in 1985.

third base, the big righty concentrated on the switch-hitting Smith, who was batting left-handed against him. On a 1–2 count, Smith lined Niedenfuer's next pitch deep and just over the right field wall for an unbelievable 3–2 victory for St. Louis. It was only the Wizard's fourteenth career homer in the big leagues.

The action switched to Los Angeles for Game Six two days later. Pitcher Orel Hershiser had a 4–1 lead going into the top of the seventh inning, thanks in part to Madlock's third home run of the series. After getting the leadoff batter, Hershiser gave up 2 runs on 3 hits before Niedenfuer was called in to put out the fire. He did, but not before giving up the tying run.

In the bottom of the eighth, Mike Marshall cracked a solo homer to the opposite field to put the Dodgers back on top, 5–4. That set the stage for one of the more thrilling rallies in league championship history.

After getting the leadoff pinch hitter, Niedenfuer gave up a single to McGee, who promptly stole second base. Smith drew a walk. Herr hit an easy bouncer to Marshall at first base, but it moved McGee to third and Smith to second. With Cardinals cleanup hitter Jack Clark coming to bat, Lasorda had to decide whether to let Niedenfuer pitch to Clark or intentionally walk him to load the bases and set up a possible force-out at any base.

The Dodgers skipper went with the percentages—righty against righty—but Clark smashed a four-hundred-fifty-foot (137.1m) home run into the left field bleachers to give the Cardinals a 7–5 lead. As he stood and watched the ball land, Dodgers left fielder Pedro Guerrero flung his glove to the ground in frustration and disgust. Four outs later, the Cardinals were NL champs.

REACHING 40—TWICE IN THE SAME YEAR

The Oakland Athletics' loss to the Los Angeles Dodgers in the World Series was about the only thing that marred the 1988 season for Oakland's José Canseco. Otherwise, the 1986 AL Rookie of the Year had the kind of season that most baseball players only dream about.

Canseco was already an established slugger, having socked a total of 64 home runs with 230

"Pardon me, I'll just take a second...base." José Canseco steals his fortieth base of the 1988 season to become the first major league player to steal 40 bases and slug 40 home runs in the same season. After he found his batting helmet, Canseco pulled up the second-base bag and held it aloft for his admirers—one of whom was probably not Brewers second baseman Jim Gantner—to see.

runs batted in over the course of his first two full seasons. But he became a more complete hitter in 1988. He cut down on his strikeouts while upping his batting average 50 points from the year before.

What made Canseco unique among major leaguers—at least through the 1995 season—is that in 1988 he smashed 42 home runs and stole 40 bases. Not Willie Mays, not Mickey Mantle, not Andre Dawson, not anyone else had ever reached the 40–40 plateau in the same season. José was the charter member of an exclusive club.

He led the league in home runs, runs batted in (124), and slugging percentage (.569), and was in the top ten in almost every offensive category, including runs, extra-base hits, and total bases. And just for good measure, Canseco cracked 34 doubles and played a solid outfield, leading the A's in assists with 11.

By the end of May, the A's were leading the AL West by 9 games over the Minnesota Twins, and Canseco had bashed 12 homers and stolen 17 bases. Those numbers were leading many observers to believe that the A's would win their division in a walk and that Canseco would become the game's first 40–40 man.

But with a mix of various slumps and injuries to several players, Oakland was felled by a June swoon. At the All-Star break the club led the division by just 5½ games over the Twins. Canseco, however, was showing no signs of slowing up, with 24 home runs and 22 steals. He was the top vote-getter in the American League for the All-Star Game.

At the end of August, Oakland's lead was back to 9 games over Minnesota. Canseco's numbers in homers and steals were 34 and 34.

On Sunday, September 18, the A's were hoping to win the rubber game of a weekend series against the Kansas City Royals. Canseco reached the first part of his dual record when he clouted his fortieth home run in Oakland's 11-inning victory. The next day, the A's clinched their division when they beat the defending World Champions, the Twins, 5–3.

On Friday, September 23, the A's opened a 3-game series against the Brewers in Milwaukee. During that game, Canseco twice stole second base to garner his thirty-ninth and fortieth thefts of the season and become the first player in big-league history to hit at least 40 homers and steal at least 40 bases. All of the few A's fans and most of

the Brewers fans in attendance gave Canseco a standing ovation as he stood at second base to acknowledge their cheers.

What made Canseco's record-breaker on the base paths so much sweeter was that he bunted safely down the third baseline to get on base. It was the slugger's first bunt of the season. Just for good measure, Canseco also smashed his forty-first homer of the season in the A's 9–8 extra-inning win over the Brew Crew. He wound up with 42 homers and 40 steals for 1988.

BULLDOG NIPS BIG D'S RECORD

The Dodgers have always been pitching-rich, whether in Brooklyn or L.A. Over the years their roster has included the likes of Burleigh Grimes, Don Newcombe, Sandy Koufax, Fernando Valenzuela, Don Sutton, Ron Perranoski, Jim Brewer, Jim Marshall, Don Drysdale, and Orel Hershiser.

It's a look that says, "Hey, choirboy this, bucko." By all accounts, Orel Hershiser is a nice guy, and he does possess what might be called the look of a choirboy. But early in his career this Gold Glover and Cy Young Award winner was nicknamed "Bulldog" for his tenacity, talent, and work ethic.

Kirk Gibson raises his fist in celebration as he rounds the bases after hitting a two-run homer in the bottom of the ninth to beat the Oakland A's in Game One of the 1988 World Series.

The last two names have a special link, because in 1968 "Big D" set a new pitching record for consecutive scoreless innings with 58. Exactly twenty years later, "Bulldog" topped that mark with 59 consecutive scoreless innings, all coming at the end of the season, when his team needed him the most: in the final stretch of its drive for the NL Western Division title.

Hershiser ended the season with 6 straight shutouts, and the Dodgers won the division by 7 games over the Cincinnati Reds. Hershiser's personal stats included tying for the league lead in wins (23) and complete games (15) and leading the league in shutouts (8) and innings pitched (267).

The Baseball Writers' Association of America named Hershiser the NL Cy Young Award winner for 1988. Of course, that award, and any other postseason award, isn't announced until after the league championship series and the World Series, both of which featured superb pitching performances by Hershiser.

He earned a rare save in Game Four of the NL championship series against the Mets at New York, then notched a 5-hit, complete shutout against them in the seventh and deciding game to propel the Dodgers into the World Series against the Oakland A's.

Against the powerful A's lineup that featured three players who blasted 24 or more home runs during the regular season, Bulldog won Game Two (a 3-hit shutout with 8 strikeouts) and the decisive Game Five (a 4-hit complete game in which he allowed only 2 earned runs while striking out nine Oakland batters).

Orel Hershiser put together what is easily one of the greatest single seasons by any major league pitcher, a season capped off by his team claiming postseason honors, but highlighted by that magnificent string of consecutive scoreless innings that helped get them there in the first place.

THE HOBBLED HERO

It took only a week for the Los Angeles Dodgers to snap up Kirk Gibson after he was granted free agency by the Detroit Tigers in early 1988. Los Angeles' front office thought its preseason acquisition could pack a punch in the middle of the lineup and provide some additional on-field leadership; an intense Gibson delivered on both counts.

The Child Is further to "The Man"

● ●

Eight year-old Nate Colbert was sitting in the stands at Sportsman's Park in St. Louis on May 2, 1954, to see a Sunday doubleheader between the Cardinals and the Giants. His favorite player, Stan "The Man" Musial, rocked the park by whacking 5 home runs and a single during the two games, en route to 21 total bases and a record. Eighteen years later, Colbert, now the first baseman for the San Diego Padres, also whacked 5 home runs in a twin bill. But he went a bit further: he hit 2 singles to his hero's 1 for 22 total bases on the day.

The thirty-one-year-old former collegiate football star hit a career high .290 with 25 homers, 28 doubles, and 76 RBI. Gibson was part of a club that possessed just the right blend of speed, power, and pitching to win their division, the NL pennant, and the World Series. Gibson wasn't the sole reason for his team's success, but he was essential to it, and his contributions in the glare of the postseason spotlight proved that.

Gibson was an 0-for-6 nonfactor early in the NL championship series. The 1986 world champion Mets rallied in the ninth inning to grab a 3–2 squeaker in Game One and the Dodgers rebounded with a 6–3 victory in Game Two.

In a rain-delayed Game Three at New York, which was decided by the Mets' 5-run outburst in the eighth, Gibson made the defensive play of the series—and one of the all-time gems in postseason history. Losing his footing on the mushy field as he broke back on a slicing liner off the bat of switch-hitter Mookie Wilson, Gibson leaped for the ball and, fully extended, caught it as he fell to the ground. Slow-motion replays show that Gibson's glove was halfway off his hand when he made the catch.

A hamstring pull had hindered Gibson throughout the playoffs, yet he was still able to turn on a Roger McDowell pitch and knock it into the stands for a dramatic twelfth-inning home run that was the difference in the Dodgers' 5–4 win in Game Four. Gibson also poked a homer in the Dodgers' 7–4 win in Game Five and a sacrifice fly in their Game Seven clincher. Despite hitting only

.154 in the playoffs, Gibson drove in 6 runs, tying him with the Mets' Darryl Strawberry for the RBI lead. By now, both of Gibson's legs hurt him.

Gibson's finest moment came in Game One of the World Series against the powerhouse Oakland A's. Trailing 4–3 and down to their last out, the Dodgers sent in pinch hitter Mike Davis to face relief ace Dennis Eckersley in the bottom of the ninth. Davis drew a walk. Some fifty-six thousand partisan fans stood and roared their approval when they saw Gibson emerge from the dugout, swing a bat, and hobble to the plate to pinch-hit.

He fouled off Eckersley's first pitch, and on his follow-through he propped himself up with his bat to avoid falling on his face.

Gibson fouled off Eckersley's next pitch, strike 2. Then he hit a little nubber up the first baseline, and winced as he ran the few feet the ball rolled before Mark McGwire scooped it up in foul territory. Gibson fought off another pitch, working the count to 2–2. Davis stole second as Gibson took ball 3. He quickly stepped out of the batter's box to ready himself, then stepped back in. Eckersley fired. Gibson swung. There was a loud crack.

The ball sailed high and far, landing well up into the right field stands. The final: Dodgers 5, A's 4. Gibson pumped his arms as he gingerly trotted around the bases. Dodger Stadium was the scene of chaotic joy.

"In a year that has been so improbable," TV announcer Vin Scully reflected on the Dodgers' season as Gibson was mobbed by his teammates at home plate, "the impossible has happened."

NOLAN'S SEVENTH NO-NO

Whatever enabled Nolan Ryan to do what he did on a baseball diamond for more than two dozen years should be bottled and sold to big-league prospects as the elixir guaranteed to ensure election to the National Baseball Hall of Fame.

Ryan was forty-four years old when the Texas Rangers broke camp in the spring of 1991, yet the man was still among the game's premier power pitchers. He was coming off a season in which he went 13–9 with a 3.44 ERA and 232 strikeouts, that last figure marking the ninth time in his career he had led the American League in Ks (he twice led the National League).

On the night of May 1, 1991, Nolan Ryan thrilled a lot of Rangers fans (not a few of whom were middle-aged) when, at the tender age of forty-four, he sent one Blue Jays hitter after another back to the bench. It was the fireballer's seventh career no-hitter.

When April 30 gave way to May 1, Ryan and his teammates were in Arlington, hosting the Toronto Blue Jays on Arlington Appreciation Night. Ryan took the mound against a lineup that included Joe Carter, John Olerud, Devon White, Kelly Gruber, and Roberto Alomar—not exactly a bunch of second-stringers. Plus, the Jays' starter was Jimmy Key, who was already 4–0 for the season. Texas was a .500 ballclub entering the game, and Ryan was pitching on four days' rest.

But the thirty-three-thousand-plus fans on hand for the game were treated to vintage Ryan. Pitch after pitch, batter after batter, inning after inning, "the Express" blew by the Jays.

In fact, the only Toronto base runners came on full-count walks: Gruber in the first and Carter in the seventh. In between came the one breathless moment when Ryan nearly lost his bid for another no-hitter. The ninth-place hitter, shortstop Manuel Lee, blooped a ball into shallow center field. Hard-charging center fielder Gary Pettis raced in and caught the ball at his knees.

In the third inning the Rangers scored all the runs their ace would need. The big blow came on Ruben Sierra's 2-run homer with Rafael Palmeiro aboard.

Throughout the night, Ryan mixed a nasty curve in with his legendary fastball to strike out at

least one Blue Jays batter in every inning on his way to notching 16 Ks. Ryan struck out the side in the third—all on curveballs. But the big story was whether Ryan would notch the seventh no-hit game of his career. The man had already become the oldest player to pitch a no-hitter when, at the age of forty-three, he mystified the Oakland A's the year before, 5–0. A mix of tension and hope was evident in the faces of Rangers fans and Ryan's teammates alike as the hurler edged closer and closer to rewriting his own history.

So when Ryan fanned Roberto Alomar on a high hard one for the third out of the ninth, the place erupted in wild celebration. Raised onto the shoulders of his teammates, a sweaty, exhausted Ryan was all smiles in the glare of the spotlight. The seemingly ageless wonder had fired a 3–0 no-hitter. Fans around the country who were watching ESPN that night saw the thrilling finish to Ryan's masterpiece when the cable network switched over from its coverage of other regional games.

Ryan finished the year at 12–6 with a 2.91 ERA (fifth in the American League) and 203 strikeouts (good for third). By anyone's standards, it was a superb year for the Express. But a seventh career no-hitter? Now that's icing.

BILL, MEET JOE

Before Game Six of the 1993 World Series, Toronto's Joe Carter told his teammates, "I've got my saddle on; hop on."

It wouldn't have been the first time the Blue Jays had ridden the slugger's back to victory. Still, few people could have predicted what Carter did to back up his promise. It was nothing short of repeating history.

Games One and Two of the Series had been fairly close affairs of 8–5 and 6–4, respectively, with Toronto winning the first game and the Philadelphia Phillies the second. Toronto easily took Game Three by a score of 10–3.

Then things got interesting.

Opposite: Broken hearts in Philly. It's the bottom of the ninth in Game Six of the 1993 World Series, and Toronto's Joe Carter follows through on his swing and his pregame promise to teammates that he'd carry them to the winner's circle. Thanks to the wretched season-ending players' strike in 1994, this would be among the last postseason images that baseball fans could cling to for some time.

The Jays scored 3 runs in the top of the first in Game Four. The Phils counterattacked with 4 runs of their own in the bottom of the first. They added 2 more runs in the second, but the Jays knocked starter Tommy Greene off the mound in the top of the third with 4 earned runs that made the score 7–6 Toronto.

The Phils tied the score in the bottom of the fourth on a single by Mariano Duncan that scored Lenny Dykstra, who had doubled. They blew the game open in the fifth on a run-scoring double by Milt Thompson that was sandwiched by a pair of 2-run homers, one by Darren Daulton and one by Dykstra.

Over the next 2 innings, both teams scored 2 runs. The Phils led 14–9 going into the top of the eighth. First Larry Andersen and then Mitch Williams gave up 3 runs, and when Williams finally recorded the third out of the frame, the stunned Phillies and their fans found themselves blinking in disbelief at a scoreboard that read Toronto 15, Philadelphia 14.

And that was how Game Four ended. At four hours and fourteen minutes, it was the longest World Series game ever played to the point. And the 29 total runs that were scored in the game broke the old mark of 22, set in Game Two of the 1936 "Subway Series" between the New York Yankees and the New York Giants. Down but not out, the Phils bounced back to win Game Five when starter Curt Schilling pitched a 5-hit gem with superb location of his pitches.

The Blue Jays led the Phils, 3 games to 2, as the Series headed back to Toronto. Game Two winner Terry Mulholland started for the Phils; Game Two loser Dave Stewart started for the Jays.

By the sixth inning, Mulholland was gone, and before Stewart could record an out in the seventh, he too was gone. That pesky Dykstra clubbed a 3-run homer against "Stew" to bring the Phils to within 1 run of the Jays, and reliever Danny Cox gave up 2 more runs that moved the Phils out in front, 6–5.

That's how things stood when the Jays batted in the bottom of the ninth. The flame-throwing Mitch Williams, called "the Wild Thing" for his on-field demeanor and occasional lack of control, walked Jays leadoff man Rickey Henderson. Devon White then flied out to left-center field. Paul Molitor—already 11 for 23 in the Series—

singled to center, sending Henderson to second with the tying run.

That brought up Joe Carter. Hitless in his previous 7 at bats, Carter had a 2–1 count when he swung at what would have been ball 3. It was a change-up low and away, and Carter was well out in front of it. Taking his lead off first, Molitor saw Daulton call for a slider. Later, Molitor would say that he thought Carter had a chance to hit the ball well if Williams made a mistake with the pitch.

He did. The ball was down the middle and above Carter's knees; it might as well have been on a hitting tee. Carter swatted the ball down the left field line and over the wall for a game-ending and Series-clinching home run.

Thirty-three years and ten days after Pirate Bill Mazeroski knocked one out of Forbes Field and made World Series history in the bottom of the ninth, Blue Jay Joe Carter saddled up at the indoor SkyDome and rode into the history books.

THE GAME'S NEW IRON MAN

Billy Ripken surely grasped the irony of his situation. There he was in Oriole Park at Camden Yards, Baltimore, on September 6, 1995, having been granted the night off to see his older brother, Cal, work. Cal hadn't had any time off in fourteen years.

Cal Ripken, Jr., made his big-league debut with the Baltimore Orioles in the strike-shortened season of 1981, garnered AL Rookie of the Year honors in 1982, the AL MVP Award in 1983 while helping the Orioles win a World's Championship, and a second MVP Award in 1991.

Early in his big-league career he alternated between third base and shortstop, for which his first big-league skipper, Earl Weaver, thought Cal was better suited. Weaver's lineup card of July 1, 1982, had Ripken penciled in at short, and since then Ripken has often led AL shortstops in putouts, assists, and fielding percentage. (He is third all-time in the last category.)

Despite playing a position that invites injury from wicked hops and sliding base runners, Ripken's talent and perseverance kept him in the lineup game after game, week after week, month after month, season after season. In fact, until

Ripken's father, then Orioles manager Cal, Sr., took him out of a lopsided game, Ripken had played more than 8,200 consecutive innings. By then, observers were saying that, barring any major injury, Ripken had a legitimate shot at breaking one of baseball's more enduring records set by one of its more endearing men: 2,130 consecutive games played, which Lou "the Iron Horse" Gehrig set in 1939.

During his quest, a determined Ripken played through the nagging cuts, bruises, and muscle pulls fated to any ballplayer, plus a severe beaning and a badly twisted right knee, both of which threatened to end his streak. But luck, blended with his dedication to, and love of, the game, helped him endure until that Tuesday evening in autumn 1995 when he tied Gehrig's mark.

The next night, the Orioles led 2–1 in the fourth, and Ripken worked the count to 3–0 off Shawn Boskie. Boskie's next pitch was a belt-high fastball that Cal ripped into the left field stands. A better script could not have been penned.

The game became official—and Gehrig's record fell—when the Angels were retired in the top half of the fifth inning. As the Orioles ran off the field, the fans rose to give Ripken a twenty-minute standing ovation. During that time, Ripken—egged on by teammates Bobby Bonilla and Rafael Palmeiro, both of whom had also homered in the game—trotted around the ballpark in a victory lap. Cal received high fives, low fives, handshakes, pats on the back, and shouts of thanks from friends, family, security guards, police, groundskeepers, umpires, the Angels team, and most especially, fans he'd never met. A nationwide television audience of millions watched him smile and say, "Thank you" to his many well-wishers.

Coming as it did a year after the ill-timed players' strike destroyed the 1994 season, Ripken's five-minute trot around the playing field was the most emotionally satisfying moment of the 1995 season. It symbolized the healing process that is still going on.

Class act: Cal Ripken, Jr., acknowledges the fans at Oriole Park at Camden Yards shortly after setting the new career record for consecutive games played. Ripken's feat did much to help the healing process in 1995 after labor strife between players and owners forced an abrupt end to the 1994 season.

Bibliography

Although a study of wire service stories and game summaries on microfilm formed the backbone of the research for this book, the following books were essential for backgrounding and cross-referencing:

Allen, Maury, *Roger Maris*. New York: Donald I. Fine, Inc., 1986.

Cohen, Richard M., and David S. Neft. *The World Series*. New York: Macmillan Publishing Company, 1986.

Craft, David, and Tom Owens. *Redbirds Revisited*. Chicago: Bonus Books, Inc., 1990.

Dickson, Paul. *Baseball's Greatest Quotations*. New York: HarperPerennial, 1992.

DiMaggio, Dom, with Bill Gilbert. *Real Grass, Real Heroes*. New York: Zebra Books, 1990.

Hynd, Noel. *The Giants of the Polo Grounds*. New York: Doubleday, 1988.

Reichler, Joseph L., ed. *The Baseball Encyclopedia* (seventh edition). New York: Macmillan, 1988.

Robinson, Ray. *Iron Horse*. New York: W.W. Norton & Co., 1990.

Index

Index

Photography Credits